Pauli Murray

The Life of a Pioneering Feminist and Civil Rights Activist

*By Rosita Stevens-Holsey
and Terry Catasús Jennings*

YELLOW JACKET
an imprint of Little Bee Books

New York, NY
Text copyright © 2022 by Rosita Stevens-Holsey and Terry Catasús Jennings
All rights reserved, including the right of reproduction
in whole or in part in any form.
Yellow Jacket and associated colophon are trademarks of Little Bee Books.
Interior designed by Natalie Padberg Bartoo and Malcolm Jamison
For information about special discounts on bulk purchases,
please contact Little Bee Books at sales@littlebeebooks.com.
Photographs and other imagery were obtained from the Schlesinger Library,
Harvard Radcliffe Institute.
Manufactured in China RRD 0921
ISBN 978-1-4998-1251-0 (hc)
First Edition 10 9 8 7 6 5 4 3 2 1
ISBN 978-1-4998-1252-7 (e)
yellowjacketreads.com

Pauli Murray

The Life of a Pioneering Feminist and Civil Rights Activist

By Rosita Stevens-Holsey
and Terry Catasús Jennings

YELLOW
JACKET

TABLE OF CONTENTS

Then let the dream linger on.
Let it be the test of nations,
Let it be the quest of all our days,
The fevered pounding of our blood,
The measure of our souls—
That none shall rest in any land
And none return to dreamless sleep,
No heart be quieted, no tongue be stilled
Until the final man may stand in any place
And thrust his shoulders to the sky,
Friend and brother to every other man.

—Pauli Murray, "Dark Testament,"
Dark Testament and Other Poems [1]

part I
....

WHY?

AN ACTIVIST IN THE MAKING

Pauli Murray never fit in.
Prickly,
she was a thorn in the side of those in power.
Her work created ladders
for others to climb
toward equality.

She was called a communist
and named a saint.
A poor child of the Jim Crow South
whom Eleanor Roosevelt came to call
friend.

A poet and a lawyer

A woman
who felt herself a man
trapped
in a woman's body.
A woman
who liked other women.
A woman
who fell in love
with other women.

Anna Pauline Murray,
who chose Pauli as her name,
never fit in.
As an outcast,
she saw both sides on matters of

race and gender.
Black
in a world where whites ruled,
she was brought up in a family of
intermingled races.
Woman
in a world dominated by men,
her skills surpassed those of the favored gender,
yet lacked the recognition
men so easily achieved.
She saw injustice and unfairness
with uncommon clarity.

And she didn't accept it.

She tried to avoid it,
sidestepping all that would humiliate her
or make her feel less than
human.
She ran away from it
when that didn't work.
But as she grew and matured,
avoiding the segregation of Jim Crow laws
and running away
didn't work.
So, she stood.
And she fought.

Her legal work became the
foundation
of the laws that brought it down.
Brought Jim Crow down.

Yet that was not enough.
Jane Crow still reigned
and women
were
still
less than.
Undeserving
of the rights of men.

So, she stood.
And she fought.
To break down
the barriers.
The barriers that held women back.

ON THE TAIL OF HALLEY'S COMET

Anna Pauline Murray arrived on the earth
November 20, 1910,
on the tail of Halley's Comet.

Her parents, Agnes and Will,
separated but reunited,
rekindled their love,
and Pauli was born.

The baby who shouldn't have been,
but was.
A child of love and reconciliation.[2]

Beautiful Agnes,
light-skinned, sunny, hot-tempered,
and selfless.
Some days,
people would say
Pauli was fiery like her mother.

Persistent Will,
quick, wiry, energetic,
and full of music.
Other days,
people would say
Pauli had her father's drive.

Pauli[3] was Sunday's child,
back then
a good omen.

Sunday's child from a nursery rhyme,
"fair and good and wise and gay."

Still, she was different.

The Murray children's world fell apart
when Pauli was barely three.
Their mother, Agnes,
died.

Will Murray became
a shadow.
Depressed.
Not stable enough to care for six children.

Only the oldest three stayed with Will,
Grace, Mildred, and Willie.
Will's sister Rose took the youngest two—
Rosetta and little Robert Fitzgerald.

Rose also wanted to take Pauli.

But, before she died,
as if warned by a crystal ball
that her own life would last no longer
than a whisper on a windy night,
Agnes, asked her sister Pauline
to take care of Pauli.

Agnes knew Pauli was different.
A rough board to be smoothed
to reveal "the fine grain of wood."[4]

She trusted no one but her sister
Pauline Fitzgerald Dame
her best friend.
Pauli's namesake.

Their connection was deep.
When Pauli was just a little over one,
Agnes, sick
and pregnant again,
left Pauli with her aunt Pauline
for nine months.
The bond they forged lasted a lifetime.

Pauline Dame knew her sister's wish.
She had lost two babies at birth
and loved Pauli as her own.
And yet,
Pauline Dame gave Pauli a choice
to live with her aunt Rose
or live with her.

Pauli Murray's choice
determined the course of her life.
She chose
Pauline Dame.

Pauli's life would have been different
with Rose Murray Shipley's clan
in Baltimore, Maryland.
Living with her siblings.
Close to her father.

She would have called her aunt Rose "Mother,"
because Rose would have insisted.
And memories
of her mother and father
would have been
erased.

Instead,
Pauline Dame took Pauli south
to Durham, North Carolina.
To a white clapboard house in a place called
the Bottoms,
where Pauli lived with the Fitzgeralds.

Her grandmother, Cornelia.
Her grandfather, Robert.
Her aunts, Pauline and Sallie.

The house in the Bottoms was
a home
where Pauli's questions about Agnes and Will
were answered.
Memories of her parents were kept alive
with stories and pictures,
that filled the void in her heart.

Even though her childhood
was tinged with a sadness she called a "gray mist,"[5]
and the knowledge of what she had lost,
Pauli found love in the house in the Bottoms.
And pride.

Aunt Pauline adopted her
and became her mother.
In fact and by law.
Pauli became her child.

Pauli came to call her "mother"
of her own choice.

THE ACTIVIST—WAS SHE BORN OR WAS SHE MADE?

One would wonder if it was
innate.
That sense of fairness
and justice
that Pauli Murray had.

Or if it was nurtured in the little house in the Bottoms.

It wasn't fair,
sometimes,
at home.

> "How come you give Grandfather *three* pancakes and me
> only one?"[6]

Asserting herself came easily.
And early.

Everyday,
Pauli went to school with Aunt Pauline,
even though she was only
four
or five.
Not old enough to be a student.
Cornelia and Robert Fitzgerald were too old
to take care of her.
Sallie Fitzgerald taught at the school as well.

In Pauline Dame's classroom,

Pauli listened
when Aunt Pauline taught her first grade class
to read.

"I can read, Aunt Pauline,"[7]
Pauli said one day
when she stood up
with the first graders,
and read.

Aunt Pauline may have thought Pauli
just remembered what other first graders had read,
so she gave Pauli a different book,
one Pauli hadn't seen before.

Pauli read every word.

She was told that a pencil belonged
in her right hand,
but it felt much better in her left.
The disapproval made her feel even more
different.
Self-conscious.

She taught herself to write with both
left and right hands.

But she didn't think it was fair
that she was the one who had to conform.

THE BOTTOMS—THE INFLUENCE OF PLACE

The activist was born
but also formed.

In the little house in the Bottoms,
her concept of family
and her concept of self
were totally different from the other five Murray children.

They were brought up in Baltimore, Maryland,
a city in the North.
Not quite as free as the state of New York,
one would say,
but still,
not North Carolina.

At first, the little house was a source of pride.
Pride of ownership
for Cornelia and Robert,
different from most Black families.
But in time,
it became
isolating.

Maplewood Cemetery
was built behind the house in the Bottoms,
with fields separating the house from the final resting place
of the whites
of Durham, North Carolina.

But as the cemetery grew,

the graves marched down the hill
until they were so near
marble angels and headstones became the closest neighbors
of the little white house.

Walking through the cemetery
was forbidden
for people of dark skin.
But Pauli decided at an early age
that a rule,
not a law,
that some white person made,
could be broken.

Maplewood Cemetery was a shortcut to everywhere,
and she used it.
But only during the day.
Ghosts,
Pauli thought,
were sure to come out at night.

Pauli talked to the newly dead.
Welcomed them to their final home.
"I knew more about the *dead* white people . . .
than the *living* ones," she said.[8]
But it wasn't by choice.

It wasn't only the cemetery
that isolated young Pauli
in the little house in the Bottoms.

An open sewer

fouled the side of the Fitzgerald property.
The waste of the city of Durham
flowed freely by their home.

Regardless of how much the Fitzgeralds asked
and pled
with those in authority
to have the city cover the ditch,
it never happened.

To the whites who made the decisions,
in Durham, North Carolina,
open sewage
by the house of a Black family
was of no concern.

Friends were hard to come by
when your house
was in front of the cemetery
and smelled
like sewage.

Friends were hard to come by
when Pauline Dame
and Sallie Fitzgerald,
your mother and your aunt,
taught at your school.

Friends were hard to come by
for a girl who liked to wear
boys' clothes
instead of girls'.

Friends were hard to come by
for a girl whose grandmother ranted
at those who neared
the little house in the Bottoms,
coloring Pauli Murray's life
with loneliness.

Outside her family,
she met very few
others.
Salesmen and tradespeople.
And even then, they were only
men.

It was in the Bottoms
that Pauli Murray learned
of Jim Crow.

Jim Crow laws
gave whites
supremacy
over people whose skin color
was dark.
Like Pauli.

Jim Crow laws
were named after a character
in a minstrel show.
A Black slave
who was lazy
and stupid.

Pauli knew that she wasn't lazy
or stupid.
And neither was her granpa,
or her granma.
Or her aunt Pauline.
Or her aunt Sallie.
No Black person she knew
was stupid
or lazy.

Yet when whites
laughed at Jim Crow in their minstrel shows,
they were laughing
at people like her
and her family.

Being laughed at
hurt.
It wasn't fair.
She hadn't chosen
the color of her skin.

Jim Crow laws
were meant to keep Black people in their
place.
Not equal.
Perhaps not slaves,
but degraded,
humiliated,
and belittled.

Inferior.

They were meant to keep Black people
away
from whites.

And they did keep
Black people
away
from whites
in the South
from the end of
the Civil War.

Because of Jim Crow,
Pauli couldn't
use the same bathrooms
as whites,
or eat in the same restaurants,
or sit next to a white person
on a train or a trolley.

Pauli attended West End School.[9]
Both elementary schools for Black children—
East End and West End—
were dilapidated, worn down.
So much so that
both ended up burned to the ground,
rumored to have been
on purpose.
The only way
to get a decent place
for Black children to go to school
was to force the whites to build a new one.[10]

Her textbooks were castoffs
from the white schools.
She never got to enjoy the smell of a new book
or hear the crack of the spine
when she was the first to open it.
Her teachers were paid
pennies on the dollar
of what white teachers earned.

Because of Jim Crow,
Pauli had to sit in the back
of all buses
and in the luggage car
when riding a train.

Because of Jim Crow,
people of dark skin
had to sit in the balcony
at the movies.
But there were no bathrooms
for them
anywhere
in the theater.

So, they had to
hold it
for the whole movie,
or leave the theater
to go to the bathroom.

Sometimes they couldn't

hold it.
So the balcony at the movie theater often smelled
like pee.

Pauli and her family avoided Jim Crow
by walking instead of riding
and not going to the movies
and always going to the bathroom
before they left home.

Small acts of
defiance.

Even being among whites on the street
was a balancing act
for Pauli.
Some white people didn't want
people of color
to look them in the eye
or walk on the same sidewalk
where they walked.

Each time Pauli met a new
white person,
she never knew who would be nice
and who wouldn't.

Mostly,
she stayed away from
white people
just in case.

But sometimes
she couldn't.

On a trip home from Baltimore
so Pauli could see her father,
Aunt Pauline slipped in the mud in front of the train station
and shattered her glasses.

Two white men stared
and did nothing
to help.

At a stop in Norfolk, Virginia,
Aunt Pauline left Pauli
guarding the suitcases in the waiting room
while she found out about the train
that would take them
to Durham.

White men with red faces
surrounded Pauli
without a word.
Until Aunt Pauline came.

It seems that the sign
Aunt Pauline wasn't able to read
through her shattered
glasses said
"White Waiting Room."

Pauli definitely was not white,
but she wasn't too dark, either.
And she confused them.

Once they got on the train,
one of the men from
the waiting room
watched them
so that Aunt Pauline and Pauli didn't
overstep
their bounds.
Again.
And sit in a place
reserved for
whites.

Jim Crow laws meant
segregation.
Meant being
separate
and different
from those who
drew white skin
in the lottery of birth.

Jim Crow meant
humiliation.

Suffering
the degradation
let Pauli understand the

injustice
and unfairness
of her lot.

Because of
nothing
but the color
of her skin.

That understanding would be
a thorn
she would always want to
pull from deep inside
her heart.

CHILDHOOD—THE INFLUENCE OF FAMILY

Upon her mother's death,
three-year-old Pauli
was thrust
into a family
of adults.

Granpa Fitzgerald
who fought for
the Union
in the Civil War.

Granma Cornelia,
the proud daughter
of a member of the
North Carolina General Assembly
and his almost-white, part-Cherokee slave.

Sallie Fitzgerald,
her always cheerful aunt.

And Pauline Dame,
her godmother,
later
her adopted mother.

All in the Fitzgerald home.

In the little white clapboard house
in the Bottoms,

Pauline Dame never sought to steal
the memory of fiery Agnes,
or driven Will.
She kept memories of Pauli's parents
alive
in pictures and stories.

"You've got your mother's sweet disposition," Dame would
say
and, "You look just like your father."[11]
Pauli would glow
at the comparisons.
She'd do her best
to make them proud.

In a home where three
of the four adults were,
or had been,
teachers, education
was bound to be the
centerpiece
of Pauli's life.

She read to her grandfather,
daily.
The newspaper.
She read the news of the
Great War
because he couldn't see
to read the paper
himself.

She also recited
words like
"ammunition" and
"preparedness"
and "conscription."

And said,
"Yes, sir,"
and
"No, sir."
Never just
"Yes" or "No,"
and never,
ever
"Yessuh" or "Nosuh."[12]

Because of Robert Fitzgerald,
his children
and grandchild
marched
everywhere
in step.
Their backbones straight.

Granpa gave Pauli
storytelling.
Reynard the Fox and the Little Red Hen
and Aesop's Fables.

When she'd been especially good,

Granpa would tell her
true stories
of his childhood
or of fighting for the Union
in the Civil War.
How he had set up schools
for Black children
in North Carolina
and how the Ku Klux Klan
rode around the little schoolhouse
to make him
stop.

She loved him,
her hero,
but Granpa Fitzgerald kept Pauli
isolated
as well.

> "I don't want you bringing stray young'uns up here," he
> told her. "I won't have every rag, tag and bobtail in the
> Bottoms cluttering up my yard."[13]

Pauli read to Granma Cornelia, too.
The Bible.
Her grandmother's
favorite book.
Because Granma Cornelia
didn't know how to read.

Pauli read on Sundays.
Psalms.

She didn't always know the
meaning
of what she read.

She skipped any word
she couldn't pronounce.

But reading
to her grandmother
brought them close.
That closeness
made Pauli the family ambassador
to Cornelia—
the cactus of the family.
Full of thorns
that might deflate
whoever
was in her way.

From the porch
of the little white clapboard house,
Cornelia Fitzgerald would
rant and rave
at anyone who dared to trespass
on her land
or looked at her wrong.

"No count,"
"Good for nothing,"
"No mannered,"
"Yaller bellied, white livered"[14]

To Cornelia,
a rattlesnake
was more respectable
than some of her
neighbors.

When her neighbors
brought up her white heritage
as an offense,
she countered.

"You think I'm insulted?" Cornelia would say. "I'll tell
anybody I'm a white man's child. A fine white man at
that. A southern aristocrat. . . . I don't like trashy folks
whether they're Black, white, blue or yaller. If you mix
with the dogs you'll be bitten by the fleas."[15]

Pauli, her favorite,
had near-magical powers
to calm her grandmother.
Pauli used the Bible
to soothe the waters.

"[Let me] read you 'Zekiel
in the valley of the dry bones,
and Dan'l in the lion's den," she'd say
and get her granma
to leave her ranting
to listen to the Bible.[16]

Pauli saw the ranting

and raving,
but she also saw
another side of her grandmother.
Bringing food
to those in need,
even when the little house
in the Bottoms
went
without.

Bringing potions
and salves
she had made
herself
to those in the Bottoms
who were ailing.

Cornelia's pride was
her white father, who
had defended poor Black people
free of charge
and had saved
many of them
from the gallows.[17]
Pauli couldn't help knowing
that as proud as Cornelia was
of her white blood,
she never mentioned the
slave blood
running through her veins.

"Hold your head high and don't take a back seat to nobody," Granma told Pauli. "You got good blood in you . . . Aristocrats . . . going back seven generations right in this state."[18]

Pauli understood
her grandmother.
She understood
her grandmother's pain,
that even though she was brought up
as part of a
white family,
upon marrying a Black man,
she became Black
and lost the privilege
and protection
from discrimination
she'd had at her father's house.
When she married Robert Fitzgerald,
Cornelia Smith lost all human rights.

She understood
her grandmother's pain,
that even though she had been
educated
by a nanny as any white girl would have been,
she lived in
the Bottoms
and few respected her.

She understood

her pain
that even though she was
seven-eighths white,
she still had to endure
the Ku Klux Klan
circling her home with torches.
Nightly.

Pauli understood.

But still.
Granma Cornelia's way
left her
isolated
in the little house
in the Bottoms.

Because of Granma Cornelia's
rants,
the neighborhood was convinced
Cornelia's evil eye
had killed a horse
and made a girl fall
pregnant.

The horse
had been eating her corn.
The girl
had let him loose.

So, Pauli

had few friends
her age.

In the house full of adults,
where children
other than Pauli
were seldom seen,
reading
became Pauli's
escape.

She didn't have
children's books,
so she read
every book
on her grandfather's shelves.
The *Works of Paul Laurence Dunbar.*
Booker T. Washington's *Up from Slavery.*
Zane Grey's adventure novels.
Gene Stratton-Porter's books on conservation.
Ellen Glasgow's books
on how the South
had changed.

She also read
Aunt Pauline's books.
Historical novels.
All books that
well-read adults
would be
proud
to have read.

When she ran out of books
in the little white house,
she trekked to
the Durham Colored Library
where the librarian introduced her
to the Bobbsey Twins,
The Five Little Peppers and How They Grew,
and *Frank the Young Naturalist.*

Once Pauli was old enough
to be in school,
friends were still
hard to come by.

She was the daughter
of Pauline Dame.
One of the strictest teachers
at Pauli's school.
And the most
respected.

Pauli wanted to be
good
but often,
wasn't.

She knew she should have been

"a model of good conduct . . . not a ringleader of
mischief." [19]

Reading,
writing,
and arithmetic
were no problem.

She excelled.

But not in behavior.
Her behavior was
not what was
expected
of a teacher's child.

Pauli bounced
when she should have been
still.
She talked
when she should have been
quiet.

Sometimes her good sense
just didn't work,
like when she sneaked away
to buy
pickles and candy
at the store next to the school.
Or when she pulled
a rotting plank
from the school fence
to make a springboard.

Once, on a rainy day,

when about a hundred students
ended up in the school basement
for recess,
Pauli organized a game
of Policeman.

Pauli ended up
bloodied.
With a gash on her forehead.
Everyone thought she was
dead.[20]

It just seemed that,
in elementary school,
whenever there was
trouble,
Pauli couldn't be far from it.

Every teacher
had a direct line
to Pauline Dame.

Pauli couldn't get away with
anything.

Pauli endured Pauline Dame's
disappointment.
Much harder to bear than any
punishment.

Pauline Dame raised Pauli
with an iron fist

wrapped
in a velvet glove.

She gave Pauli
choices.
Chores she had to do,
but Pauli got to
choose
how she would
help.

Picking the fruits of the
garden and orchard.
Helping tend the vegetable garden.
She helped with the chickens
and stacking wood,
kept oil in the lanterns
and coal in the scuttles.
She even scrubbed the outhouse
and swept the porch.

Cooking and sewing
were chores she never
chose.

There was only
enough
in the little white house
to live on,
but no more.

Pauli was expected to

work for her spending money,
but she could
decide
how she would earn it.

She worked
after she finished her chores.
She sold magazines
and delivered newspapers.
She swept a neighborhood store
and helped her Aunt Sallie with housekeeping.
Black children didn't earn a lot
when they worked
in Durham, North Carolina,
and it would take her until high school
to earn enough money
to buy a bike.

PROUD SHOES—THE INFLUENCE OF HERITAGE

Pauli lived with the
legends
of the Fitzgerald family
blended
with Murray family lore
every day
of her life.

They became a mosaic
embedded in her soul.

Those stories created
pride.
Pride that was the rudder
that would steer her ship.
Pride that gave her the sense
she was a human being.
Equal to all others.
Regardless
of the color of her skin.

That pride gave her the
understanding
that although others would want
to humiliate her,
they didn't have the
right.

That pride gave her the strength

to endure.
To fight.

Pauli Murray stood tall
in proud shoes.[21]

She grew up with the stories of
Robert Fitzgerald,
who changed from the Union Army
to the Union Navy
and then back again
by lying
and saying that he could see
when he couldn't
after he was wounded
driving a wagon during
a battle.

"My grandfather was a soldier for the Union and fought
for freedom."[22]

That's what Pauli told anyone
who bragged about
anything.
And that
was the end
of that.

There was nothing as important,
or as awe-inspiring,
as having fought for

freedom,
and Pauli knew it.

Pauli knew that
Robert Fitzgerald
fought with the 5th Massachusetts.
A new regiment,
Black soldiers all,
under white officers.

They took a fortification
and a howitzer gun
at Petersburg, Virginia.
The regiment proved
that Black soldiers
weren't lazy
or cowards.

Granpa Fitzgerald's musket
and his saber,
his bayonet
and his pistol,
were always kept under his bed.
Monuments
to his worth.[23]

Pauli never forgot
what Robert Fitzgerald told her
about how he felt.

How he felt when
Abraham Lincoln

signed
the Emancipation Proclamation.

It was the earthquake
that remade his life.
Finally, Abraham Lincoln proclaimed
he was a
man.
Like all others.
Despite
the color of his skin.

Slavery was abolished
in states that fought against the Union.
And soon thereafter,
the passage of the Thirteenth Amendment
ended slavery
once and for all in the whole United States.
No man
could ever again
own
another man.

Throughout his life
through his service for the Union,
Robert Fitzgerald's overwhelming dream
was to be able to
vote.
To vote and have
a say
in how his country was run.
It was a right he didn't get

until five years
after the end of the war.
And even then,
it was a tenuous right.
Easily taken away
from many persons
of black skin
by the poll tax
or
by literacy tests.

> This is our portion, this is our testament,
> This is America, dual-brained creature,
> One hand thrusting us out to the stars,
> One hand shoving us down in the gutter.[24]

Pauli heard
Cornelia Fitzgerald's stories
of how she was brought up
by her white aunt,
Mary Ruffin Smith,
and educated
by a white nanny.

But Mary Ruffin Smith
donated all of Cornelia's inheritance
to the University of North Carolina
and to the church
because of the
slave blood
that ran within Cornelia's veins.

Pauli hurt
for her grandmother
and what she had
endured—
a hurt that never left her.

Will's and Agnes's stories she heard
secondhand
from Aunt Pauline.
She learned of her parents'
loving relationship.
How they volunteered
in settlement houses
and helped the community.

She learned how her mother
defied her parents' wishes
and became a beloved nurse.

And her father's hard work
as a teacher
and a principal,
a man who worked
tirelessly
to better himself.
A man who made sure his students learned
life skills,
not just learning from books.
He even taught them science.
Unheard of
for Black students.

She learned of her mother's efforts
to help him heal
from typhoid.
The illness that
robbed him
of his mind.

Pauli only met her father
once
in an insane asylum.
Someday,
she told herself,
she'd spring her father
free.[25]

Pauline Dame's story
was the most significant to Pauli.

Dame was so
light-skinned
she could
pass
for white.

She married a blue-eyed man
who could pass, too.
A smart lawyer
who would stay poor
as a Black man,
but had a good chance at being rich
if he passed
for white.

Aunt Pauline didn't want to give up
her family
and her heritage.
She did not want to
pass.

Her husband left
and never came back.

The Fitzgerald and Murray stories
sustained Pauli.

It was Robert Fitzgerald's
legacy
that would urge Pauli to
persevere
and fight.
Like him.
For her rights
and those of others.
Against all odds.

It was Cornelia's
legacy
that helped her understand
the effect of even
a drop
of slave blood
coursing through a person's veins.

Will's and Agnes's drive to help others

would become her own.
But Aunt Pauline's choice
was the beacon
that guided Pauli's life.

Aunt Pauline was proud of her race
and her heritage.
And she was understanding
of what she called Pauli's
boy/girl thing,
never squelching it.
She never pushed Pauli away
from the calling of her body.

Because of Pauline Dame,
Pauli never felt ashamed
of her feelings
or her race.
She never gave in.
No matter the insult.
No matter the injury.
No matter the hurt of feeling out of place
in her own skin.

Pauli not only learned
the price
of the color of her skin,
but she came to understand
that heritage
was priceless.

Pauline Dame would be Pauli's
mentor,
model,
and guide.

Pauline Dame molded Pauli
into a woman with a deep sense
of self and
fairness.
Someone who would fight for justice
for her race.
And for her gender.

On Mother's Day,
Pauli would wear
a white flower
to honor her dead mother,
and a red one
to honor Pauline Dame.

SHADES—THE INFLUENCE OF COLOR

Color
was the defining quality of Pauli Murray's life.
Like it was for all people of her race.

There was dark skin.
And caramel-colored skin.
And light skin.
And almost-white skin.
All in Pauli's family.

Like tree bark, she said:
    "Ebony, bamboo, cocoanut, mango."[26]
Pauli knew
the family pecking order
was set by
the color of one's skin.

She, herself,
the comingled mixture
of European,
African,
and Native American stock.

Her grandfather Fitzgerald,
son of a half-Irish Black man
and a white woman
who was French and Swedish.
Grandmother Cornelia, one-eighth Black.
The rest white, with a little Cherokee.

Pauli's generation
was light-skinned.
Although Pauli
was the darkest of them all.

Even though she was dark within her family,
in the rainbow of human skin color,
hers was still light.
Yet to whites,
Pauli was unmistakably
colored.

On a shopping trip,
a light-skinned relative asked Pauli
to stay outside the store.
She'd get better service,
she knew,
without the
hindrance
of a dark-skinned child
by her side.

Pauli never forgot these
experiences.
They etched themselves
onto her soul.

Some folks in Pauli's family
"passed."
They passed for white.

They passed so well
they were never heard from
again.

Others lived as whites
most of the time
but came home for holidays,
weddings, and funerals.

Who could blame light-skinned people
for passing
if they could?
Why endure
the humiliation?
And injustice?
Why put yourself in danger?

Pauli knew the stories well.
From Granma Cornelia,
when she was young
and just married.
The Ku Klux Klan
rode around the house
she and Granpa Fitzgerald had built.
They came late at night,
while Granpa Fitzgerald was still at work
and Granma was alone.
The Klan came on horses
with torches.
They threatened
to burn the Fitzgerald home
to the ground.

Cornelia Fitzgerald was so afraid
she walked twelve miles to town[27]
in the dark
rather than
chance
being burned to death.
Alone.
In her own home.

Pauli heard of a woman
who died
because of
the color of her skin.
She was in a car accident
and died
on the way to a colored hospital
miles away.
A white hospital nearby
could have saved her.
But that hospital
refused.[28]

Pauli saw John Henry Corniggins
lying in a field
with blood
everywhere
and a fly
lingering
on his lips,
then passing slowly
into his mouth.

His brother
crying.

His mother
screaming.

The white man said
John Henry Corniggins
stole
a watermelon.
But there was no watermelon
by John Henry's body.
And John Henry's brother
didn't have a watermelon.
And the watermelon field
was way uphill
from where John Henry
lay.

He and his brother only ran
through a corner of the white man's field.[29]

How could Pauli Murray
ever cross that field
again
and not remember
John Henry Corniggins?

And his brother's
cries?

And his mother's
screams?

How could Pauli Murray
ever cross that field
again
and not wonder
what if it'd been her
instead of John Henry Corniggins
crossing that field
that day?

It was not just
dangerous,
it was unjust.
John Henry Corniggins's death
went unpunished.
As if his death
had no importance.

The white man was not arrested,
tried,
or sentenced
for the murder he'd committed.

When Pauli was 13,
a white orderly
who beat Pauli's father
with a baseball bat,
beat him 'til he died,
only got ten years in prison.
Ten years

is what her father's life was
worth.

Because his skin was
dark.

She was twelve when he died.
She never got to spring her father free.

She would only ever know him
through borrowed memories.
The most unfair blow of all.

The color of her skin meant
danger.
The color of her skin meant
fear.
But the color of her skin was something
over which she had no control.

As a child, Pauli Murray had tried to avoid
Jim Crow
whenever she could,
like she saw Pauline Dame and her aunt Sallie do.
But for Pauli Murray,
avoiding Jim Crow
was not enough.

One day she would go North,
she thought.
Where Jim Crow didn't live.

Where there were no laws
to make her feel
less than human.
Where she wouldn't have to be afraid.
And no one would care
about the color of her skin.

Pauli Murray's maternal grandparents, Robert George and Cornelia Smith Fitzgerald, 1910.

75-year-old Robert George Fitzgerald in his army uniform taken at Soldiers Home Hampton Virginia, 1912-1915.

Portrait of Agnes Fitzgerald Murray and William H. Murray, 1908-1911.

The Fitzgerald daughters. Seated, left to right: Roberta Annetta Fitzgerald, Mary Pauline Fitzgerald, and Maria Louise Fitzgerald. Standing, left to right: Agnes Georgianna Fitzgerald, and Sallie Fitzgerald. 1895-1898.

Pauli Murray as
a toddler, 1913.

Pauli Murray, seated, 1927 for
her high school graduation.

Portrait of Pauli's aunt Pauline
Fitzgerald Dame at about the
time that Pauli came to live with
her, 1910-1915.

House in the Bottoms where Pauli Murray
grew up: 906 Carroll Street, Durham, NC

part II

················

THE RELUCTANT ACTIVIST

TRYING TO GET AWAY—HUNTER COLLEGE

College in New York had been her goal.
To get away from
Jim Crow.
To get the education
Robert Fitzgerald had said
was the key to
emancipation.

Aunt Pauline agreed,
even though Pauli had no money.
Aunt Pauline agreed,
even though Pauli received a scholarship
to a local Black college.

It was a daunting task
to even find a school
in New York
she could attend.

There were many colleges and universities
in New York City
in 1926,
but most did not teach humans
born into the female gender.

Looking for freedom from
Jim Crow
in New York,
sixteen-year-old Pauli found a different kind of
oppression.

Being female
denied her opportunities
which should have been
hers.

Hunter College broke the mold.
It taught women,
and it was free
for residents of the state of New York.

Pauli needed a place to live.
To some way connect her
to the state of New York
so her tuition would be
free.

Pauline and Pauli called
on relatives
and friends
in New York
to help Agnes and Will's little girl
achieve her dream
of education
away from Jim Crow.

Aunt Pauline's cousin
Maude
answered the call.
A friend of Agnes's.
Another woman
who had lost a daughter at birth.
She invited Pauli to live in her home

in New York
for a year.
Anything
to help Pauli escape Jim Crow
and to further the education they all knew
was the only path to
freedom.

Maude legally adopted Pauli
and at seventeen,
she became eligible
to enter Hunter College.

But even with Maude's help,
the path to Hunter College was
rocky.
Jim Crow's claws reached all the way to New York City
to try to stop her.

Pauli hadn't learned enough
in the colored schools
in Durham, North Carolina,
to even apply.

In North Carolina,
Black children were only allowed to attend
eleven grades
before graduating,
while white children
went for twelve.

The books she'd used

were castoffs
from the white kids' schools.
Tattered
and out of date.

Her teachers
earned less than two-thirds
of what white teachers earned.
They,
themselves,
had only learned
what Jim Crow schools had to offer.

Pauli's grammar was atrocious,
the only poems she'd ever read
were Dunbar's poems when she was a child.
Being first in class
in a colored school
in Durham, North Carolina, meant
nothing.

Even though she'd attended eleven years of school,
Pauli's education lacked
two years'
worth of subjects
according to the state of New York.

Maude only offered
one year's
lodging.

Pauli crammed two years

into one
at Richmond Hill High School
by teaching herself
and testing out.
The state of New York required students
to pass Regents exams
to graduate.
Pauli sat in on courses
to listen
and learn
in addition to the classes
in which she was enrolled.
The plan was to take Regents exams in both
the classes she sat in on
and the classes she was enrolled in.

She was competing with white students
for the first time.

Anxious.
The only Black student
in a school of four thousand.[30]
Wondering whether it was true
that she was inferior
because she was
Black.

She struggled in classes like math,
but she excelled in physics
where everyone was taking the subject
for the first time.

Cramming
and studying
didn't leave time for Pauli to help Maude around the house.
Not that she would have wanted to.
Picking up and cleaning
would have been her least favorite thing
in the whole world.
And she had an excuse:
She needed to study.

Maude had counted
on Pauli's help
in return for her generosity.
It became a problem for Maude,
but not as big a problem
as Pauli's color.

Maude's neighbors treated their family
differently.
They stopped talking to them
and coming over
once Pauli moved into her house.

It wasn't passing
on purpose,
what Maude and her family did.

It had just happened.
They were the first
in the neighborhood.
Accepted as white,
and the subject of

race
was never discussed.

Denying her race was something Pauli
had never done.

That's not what Aunt Pauline had taught her.
Pauli would never be ashamed
of her race.
She would never deny
her heritage.

She understood what Maude did
to get along in her world.
But it chafed Pauli
at every turn.

Tensions in the house ran high,
but this was Pauli's only chance
to get a good education.

Chafing or not,
both Maude and Pauli
endured.

In New York, Pauli made a discovery.
The New York Times called people of dark skin
"Negro"
with a capital N,
not a little n,
like in the South

or the other n-word,
which was even
worse.

Negro is a race.
It is a word
heavy with dignity.

She was proud
to be a Negro
with a capital N
even though at Maude's house,
she had to pretend
otherwise.

Pauli passed every single
Regents examination.
She graduated
again
in just one year
from Richmond Hill High School
in New York
with honor.[31]

Cousin Maude agreed
to one more year of lodging
so Pauli could enter the freshman class
at Hunter College
that fall.

After a year at Richmond Hill

she was not as prepared
nor nearly half as smart
as she thought herself to be.

At Hunter College
her English composition and writing grades were as low
as any she had ever earned,
a dire situation
for a person who hoped to be
a writer.
The lack of confidence she felt
and the low grades she earned
were hard to bear
for a person who had always been
first
in her class.

She had help from Miss Reigart,
a teacher
who believed in her.
Who invited Pauli for tea at Christmas.
Pauli's grades for Miss Reigart rose slowly
through the semester,
from D- to B,
with her last grade
being an A.

She had help from Lula Burton
a Black student,
one of the few at Hunter College.
Lula,
from the North,

who, by being just as intelligent and accomplished
as the whites in her class,
dispelled
the Jim Crow myth.
They met as freshmen
and shared a love of words.
Lula tutored Pauli
in English composition,
Miss Reigart's class,
and introduced her to poets
like Frost, and Sandburg, and Edna St. Vincent Millay.
And became her friend.

Because of Lula,
Pauli came to understand that it wasn't race
and it wasn't color
that kept people of dark skin
from achieving.

It was lack of
preparation
and schooling.

These
she could overcome.

A little bit more help
allowed Pauli to get through Hunter College.

She had help from Susie Elliott,
her cousin,
who got her a job at the YWCA

so she could leave Maude's house.
Avoid the guilt she felt
at freeloading.
Live on her own.
Completely on her own.

But living on her own
had its downsides.

A roof over her head
and food on the table
were not guaranteed.
It was all up to her
working wherever she could,
at jobs that would be there one day
and gone the next,
victims of the Great Depression.

Pauli managed to make ends meet.
Sometimes.
Skipping meals,
walking everywhere,
getting clothes from the faculty discard closet.
Living for more than a week
on hominy grits with butter
"borrowed"
from her landlady.

She had to leave school for a year
for lack of funds.
Hunger and loneliness drove her into a relationship
with a boy,

William (Billy) Roy Wynn.[32]
The relationship
became a marriage
because her religious beliefs
demanded it.
And both were so poor, neither
could afford
to leave the place where they slept.
He the basement of the building where he worked,
she the Y.
As a married couple they would both be
kicked out.

But for Pauli it was just as well.
Living apart.
Immediately she found
she was repulsed by the physical
part of marriage
to a man.
Something in her fought
against it.
What she wanted from a man was
comradery, not romance.[33]
Frustrated,
living apart
and in secret,
the marriage only lasted months.
Pauli had it annulled several years later.
"A dreadful mistake."[34]

It was a time when Pauli learned,
really learned,

what it meant to be
poor.

Still,
Pauli loved everything about New York.
From the Statue of Liberty
to the Automat,
where a nickel in a slot
could buy you a hot dinner
from a rotating carousel behind glass.

But even in New York,
when she least expected it,
Jim Crow would reach out
and knock her down.

Her job at an Alice Foote MacDougall restaurant
included food as part of her pay.
Pauli and other Black workers
were given leftovers
in the basement.
The white staff
ate upstairs
with the customers
and ordered from the menu.

When out to eat at a restaurant by herself,
she always waited
anxiously
until a glass of water
and a menu
were in front of her at the table.

Proof
that she'd be allowed to stay.

Outside of Harlem,
her seat at the movies
might be behind
a pole.
Signs proclaimed,
"Double Feature tonight
—Negroes upstairs!"

Job want ads said,
"Help Wanted
—Whites only need apply!"[35]

A job at a girls' camp was denied one summer
because no counselors with Black skin
were wanted for that job.

It was a blow to Pauli, that rejection,
because the job
was at a YWCA camp.
A Christian camp
whose managers should behave with
compassion
and understanding,
not discrimination.

The first step toward activism for Pauli
came at Hunter College.

The history of Black people,

she learned at Hunter College,
was all
wrong.

Black people,
according to her history teacher,
had made no contributions
to the national progress
other than being
the object of the war
over slavery.
In that war
they were on the wrong side.
That history of Black people
made Pauli feel
ashamed.

She knew in her bones
that history was different,
but she couldn't raise a challenge.

No one had taught her the history of Black people
in school
in Durham, North Carolina.
And to the history teacher at Hunter College,
Pauli was
invisible.

Knowing the true history of her people
became a passion.

Letting others know

the true history
would become a mission.

She and a friend tried to organize
the few Black students
to share ideas and knowledge
about their background
and their race.

It was meant to be a way to learn
and bond.
But Black people were a tiny minority at the school.
Providing a forum for Black students
and only Black students
was too big a step
at Hunter College.

Student government leaders
merged the discussions on the Black race
into the International Student Union.

It was bound to fail.

Few white students were interested in the discussions.
Black students were not interested,
again,
in being a minority
in a group with no idea how they felt.

The failure was a lesson
Pauli would never forget.

Hunter College was the hardest time of her life.
Money was never enough.
Nor was food.
Jobs came and went.
Yet Pauli persevered,
survived,
and thrived.

It made a writer out of her.

> "I had always had an interest in writing. I had been
> writing on tablets from the time that I was a little tot.
> I even wrote a novel by the time that I was thirteen or
> fourteen. A horrible thing . . . *The Angel of the Desert* . . .
> the most stereotyped thing. The heroine, wouldn't you
> know, was blonde with blue eyes, golden hair, you know,
> a real little sort of Evangeline or whatever you want to
> call her, a Little Eva. The wicked sister was a brunette
> with dark hair."[36]

The novel was published
one summer in serial form
by Louis Austin of *The Carolina Times*,
a newspaper where
Pauli had worked
over the years
doing everything from
janitorial
to editing work.

At Hunter she majored in English.
She tried to take nothing

but writing courses.
Her poetry was published
in the school literary magazine.
Education,
her family's profession,
did not interest her.

For Miss Reigart, Pauli wrote the seeds
of what would become
Proud Shoes,
not only an epic history of her family,
but a primer
on the history of the Black race.

It was the first time
she'd felt free
to talk about something
so precious to her.
Her heritage.
And Miss Reigart recognized the
spark
of creativity
in her work.

Recognition.
Encouragement.
What Pauli needed.

A summer trip to help a friend
drive to California
provided her with inspiration.

"Song of the Highway"[37]
spoke of the song
that lingered in her heart
after the trip.

    I am the Highway,
    Long, white, winding Highway,
    Binding coast to coast
    And people to people;
    I am the spine of the earth.

    Over the hills I glide
    And then, come swooping down
    To some deserted spot.
    Over river and lake I stride—
    Through farm and field, and town,
    Through desert sands, white-hot.

    I laugh when the brooklets laugh,
    And weep with wayside trees
    So bent—so broken by the wind.
    Sometimes the birds and flowers
    Fill my path with song and bloom;
    Sometimes a fragrant breeze
    Leaves me drenched with faint perfume.

    I hear the sounds of earth—
    The low of cattle on the plains,
    Clatter of hoof, sound of horn,
    Rustling fields of rye,
    Of wheat, of tasseled corn;

Sweet sounds, so dear—
As through the year
Life marches on.

I am old—sad things I know,
Ache of road-worn travelers,
Lonely hours; the tragedy of pioneers
Who trudged through scorching lands,
Through rain—and snow,
Who bartered with famine—thirst—
And death—to give me birth.

But I go on in silence,
For those who know my life
Will sing my song,
Song of the Highway,
Long, white, winding Highway.

But the trip to California for fun
ended as soon as she arrived
when a letter from Aunt Pauline
forwarded from New York
was waiting for her.
Aunt Pauline was sick.
Aunt Pauline needed her home.
In Durham, North Carolina.

Pauli had no money for train fare,
neither did Aunt Pauline.
Riding freight trains
without paying

was her only option.

To get to Aunt Pauline, Pauli
hopped on trains,
already-moving trains,
trying not to end up under the wheels,
trying to avoid the guards
who would shoot her on sight.

She slept in hobo cities
under bridges
near railroad yards
dressed in her scout outfit,
pretending
to be a boy
this time
in hopes of being safe,
not acting out her preference for the masculine.

She rode in cattle cars,
cars carrying fruit and butter.
She rode for eighteen hours
in an empty refrigerator chest
with a tiny trapdoor
which could slam shut
and trap her
without air
and food
for days.
She lived on oranges
she stole from a crate.

Aunt Pauline
wasn't nearly as sick
when Pauli arrived
as she'd feared from the letter that caused her to return.

"Three Thousand Miles on a Dime in Ten Days,"
an essay,
was born from that return trip.
Pauli spoke of a boy,
Pete, who rode with her.
Yet the picture of Pete
was Pauli
dressed in her scout outfit.
And the introduction to the essay
tells that
the two of them started
with a dime.
Really.
With a dime.
To get to his mother
who was "desperately ill."
And the experience was
harrowing
in the essay.
Poetic license. [38]

But it earned her a place
along with literary stars
of the time.
"Three Thousand Miles on a Dime in Ten Days"
crowned with "Song of the Highway"
was published in 1934

in an anthology called *Negro*,
a book about Black people,
and their art,
written by prominent white and Black writers.
Pauli's essay appeared
along with the work
of Langston Hughes,
Zora Neale Hurston,
Ezra Pound,
and William Carlos Williams.

Pauli.
The writer.
Graduated one of
four
Black women
in Hunter College's class of 1933.

She had not been able to avoid Jim Crow,
but she had managed to
survive
despite its cruelty.

Now Pauli was on her own.

In the middle of the Great Depression,
segregation took on an even uglier face.

ACTIVISM FORGED ON THE ANVIL
OF THE GREAT DEPRESSION

Pauli had always thought that
college
would be a stepping-stone,
to the success Granpa Fitzgerald
had promised.

Not a guarantee,
but a step.

But by her graduation
from Hunter College in 1933,
the Great Depression erased
every shred of
hope
Pauli might have had
to get ahead.

It made everyone
equally likely
to be
unemployed.

Pauli felt lucky
to have a job.
Even if it was answering calls at the switchboard
of Hunter College,
despite the fact she had a college degree.
She was the first employee of color

not in the janitorial service.
But at least her job at the switchboard
came with a benefit.
Poetry.
Which she wrote in between answering calls.

The Great Depression
raged.
Money was scarce.
And work was
stressful.
So stressful
Pauli became sick.
Malnutrition had plagued her in school,
for lack of money.
Now it was pleurisy.
Her doctor was afraid tuberculosis
was around the corner
if she didn't take time
to heal.

The doctor said Pauli needed rest
and sun.
Not work.
But how?
A woman's camp on Bear Mountain
in New York
where outdoor life and square meals ruled
was the doctor's recommendation.
But Pauli had to be unemployed to qualify.
She didn't have a choice.

She needed to quit work
to get better.

Camp Tera,
Part of the Federal Emergency Relief Administration,
was the brainchild of Eleanor Roosevelt.
One of twenty-eight camps[39]
that provided
refuge
and healing.
A place meant to rebuild
bodies and minds
of broken
and unemployed women,
like Pauli.

It was not all that unusual
for unemployed women
in the Depression
to take advantage
of the camps—
homeless shelters of the time—
with full access to the outdoors.

At Camp Tera,
Pauli found her friend
Pee Wee Inness.
A friend from her time at the Y.
They became roommates.
Pee Wee wrote letters
when she saw

injustice.
Letters in her "distinctive narrow, perpendicular script."[40]
Pee Wee wrote public officials
and even the First Lady, Eleanor Roosevelt,
about injustice
and got answers back.

> "I owe to Pee Wee's example my later habit of writing to
> newspapers and public figures on social issues, letters I
> came to call 'confrontation by typewriter.'"[41]

At Camp Tera, Pauli's cough
disappeared
and she gained weight.
But Camp Tera
had another benefit.

Peg Holmes was a counselor
who liked Pauli's poetry
and hikes in the woods.

She liked
Pauli Murray.
Even though Pauli was poor
and Black
and Peg was a banker's daughter.
And white.
She seemed to like Pauli Murray in the way
a woman would like a man.

Camp Tera should have been heaven

for Pauli
and a haven
from the stress of the poverty she was
enduring.
And it was,
for three months.

But it all
fell apart
when Eleanor Roosevelt
visited Camp Tera.

Pauli washed her face
and put on a clean white shirt.
But when Mrs. Roosevelt passed by,
Pauli acted like she was reading.
She did not look up.

And the camp director
noticed.

Mrs. Roosevelt, Pauli told the camp director,
didn't want any bootlickers.

But perhaps
Pauli had made her first
political statement.[42]
In Pauli's eyes,
President Roosevelt could put an
end
to the oppression of Black people

in the South
and to lynching.
But he hadn't.
White Southern votes were more important to him
than Black lives.

She had taken another step toward activism.
A step to protest
the treatment of her race.

It was a bold step
for an unemployed woman
who had
nothing
and was dependent on the government
and Camp Tera
for
everything.

She stood up to
authority
for the first time
living by her convictions
at a time
when survival
was the only thing that
mattered.
She made a quiet gesture
against injustice and mistreatment.

The director of Camp Tera
watched Pauli

with an eagle eye.
And searched her cabin.
Soon after,
she kicked Pauli out.
She kicked Pauli out
because she did not look up
at Mrs. Roosevelt.
And because she found a book
by Karl Marx
in Pauli's room
from a class Pauli took
in college.

Only a
communist
would have such a book in her room.
At least, that's what the director said.

But maybe the director kicked her out
because she didn't like
that Peg Holmes was
white
and Pauli Murray was
Black
and they were
two women
and they loved
each other.

Still unemployed,
and without a place to live,
Pauli slept in a friend's studio

in an office building in New York
and used the public bathroom
to wash herself
and her underwear
after all the office workers had gone
home.

She brought up pails of water
to cook
on a two-burner stove
while she looked at the want ads
for the next day.

Peg Holmes followed her
to New York
a month later
and at the friend's apartment
their friendship and
love deepened.[43]
With nothing else to do,
for five weeks
they hitchhiked from New York
across the country
to Nebraska.
Another bold step for Pauli,
to show the preference toward
the masculine
her body demanded.
Pauli wore her scout uniform.
This time not as a shield
from men's advances,
but as a statement

of her gender preference.
They slept in courthouses
and anywhere
they didn't have to
pay.

Sometimes
they got breakfast for free.
Other times,
they worked.
Mowing lawns or doing chores
for their meals.
They even spent a night in jail,
the only safe place they could find.
The total funds between them
at the end of the trip:
80 cents.

There was nothing
Pauli would have liked more
than to continue
the relationship with Peg Holmes
beyond the trip.
Way beyond the trip.
But it was not to be.
After Pauli confessed her deep feelings,
Peg found that she could not return them
in the same way.
Years later Pauli met Pet again—Peg
was married to a man
and had children.

Pauli found that
the Great Depression
continued to teach.
Perhaps not the education that Robert Fitzgerald
would have wanted for Pauli,
but an education that would mold her
and allow her to
understand
from personal experience
what it was to be
poor.

At last, she found a job.
The Works Progress Administration (WPA)
became the textbook
for Pauli's education as an
activist.

Her job:
Teaching men and women
and children of immigrants,
both Black and white,
to read.

She heard echoes
of Jim Crow in their stories.
Treated as
inferior
and unworthy
and incapable
not because
of the color of their skin,

but because
of where they came from.

But unemployment didn't differentiate
between Blacks or whites.
Americans or foreigners.
It mowed down
everyone
in its path.

Oppression found the poor
no matter what the color.

> I was an Israelite walking a sea bottom,
> I was a Negro slave following the North Star,
> I was an immigrant huddled in ship's belly,
> I was a Mormon searching for a temple,
> I was a refugee clogging roads to nowhere—
> Always the dream was the same—
> Always the dream was freedom.[44]

Pauli met radical intellectuals.
Union organizers.
Young people who,
like she,
wanted to fight
for the welfare
of all those who
struggled.
She saw the parallels
between the treatment of the Negro in the South
and the Nazi treatment of Jews in Germany.[45]

"It seems to me that the testing ground of democracy and Christianity in the United States is in the South; that it is the duty of Negroes to press for political, economic and educational equality for themselves and for disinherited whites; that it is the responsibility of socially-minded Negro and white Southerners to work out this problem; and that the job of interpretation and leadership falls to those of both races with a knowledge of the problems and an understanding of the tremendous task to be accomplished."[46]

These are the thoughts that pushed Pauli
on a new path.
The path
of social work.
To help make the changes
that would lead
to the end of
oppression.

Another step
toward social activism.[47]

FIRST STEPS

A degree in social work
would allow Pauli to help those
who were
oppressed
and help them find
a leg up
and perhaps
a better life.

Being a social worker
would allow Pauli to help
people like those
she had been teaching.

She could have stayed in New York,
and found a school there, but
Aunt Pauline was sixty-eight.
Aunt Sallie was widowed and penniless.
As well as taking care of strangers,
Pauli thought,
she should take care of her own.

Pauli chose to return to the South,
back to the state where she was brought up,
back to the state where she had to watch
where she walked on the street
and who she talked to.

Where John Henry Corniggins had been
murdered.

And where she still had to ride
in the back of the bus.

Back to the place where little
had changed
since she had left,
except for the lives of those she loved.

The call from her loved ones was strong.

The University of North Carolina
had a graduate school for social work.
Howard Odum,
a white man
who had determined the fate of Black people
at the beginning of the century
with his books on their inferiority,
and his theories
about how Black people could never
improve,
was at that university.
His stance had
evolved.
He was now
a champion of her race.

What better teacher could she find?

If she endured
the segregation of the South,
Pauli might be able to

both
help her aunts
and achieve her goal.

But no Black person had
ever
been a student at the grand university[48]
for which Cornelia's ancestors
had donated land,
where Pauli's great-great grandfather
had been a trustee,
and her great-grandfather and his brother
had attended.

No Black person had
ever
been a student at the grand university
where Mary Ruffin Smith
had donated
Cornelia Fitzgerald's inheritance.

But the *Gaines* decision
in the Supreme Court
weeks before she decided to apply
had guaranteed Black people
the right
to higher education.
In December of 1938,
the Supreme Court had ruled that
the state of Missouri
must provide Lloyd Gaines—
a Black man—

with the opportunity for an education in law.
A separate opportunity,
but equal,
to that which was provided to whites.
Or
Lloyd must be allowed to enter
the University of Missouri School of Law.

The *Gaines* decision was a door that was already open.
They couldn't deny her,
could they?

Of all people,
shouldn't she be the first
Black human
to attend
the University of North Carolina?

A CRUEL BLOW

The answer was . . .
no.

The University of North Carolina
did not accept her.

The racist outcry
from students,
legislators,
and the press,
was crushing.
Even someone who should have known better,
Dr. James E. Shepard,
president of the North Carolina College for Negroes,
disagreed.
Negroes would do their best work among their own,
he said.
The state of North Carolina
should provide a separate law school
for Black people.

Aunt Pauline was frightened at the outcry.
Afraid
whites would burn her house down.
Afraid
that Pauli's challenge
would result in her dismissal
from her job
without retirement
or pension.

The university hid behind the constitution
of the state of North Carolina
saying that whatever was provided
for the Negro
must be
separate.

Pauli countered in a letter.
The constitution
of the state
of North Carolina
was "inconsistent"[49]
with the Constitution of the United States.
Confrontation by typewriter.

The Black press covered the arguments
on both sides,
whereas the white press
mostly covered the cons.

And the NAACP
did not take her case.

Thurgood Marshall was the one to turn her down.
Pauli
was not a resident of North Carolina,
although the school did admit out-of-state students.
The NAACP chose their candidates
only
after "meticulous scrutiny into background, training, and
personal circumstances."[50]

The NAACP couldn't afford to take on a case
they couldn't win.

Pauli
accepted their decision.

> "Here is a part of the contradictions in my personality
> where I am extremely individualistic, but at the same
> time have a very strong sense of team play and you
> know, if the National NAACP did not feel that they
> could take the case, I would hesitate and think a long
> time before I would sort of 'go off the reservation,' so to
> speak."[51]

But rejection
was a bitter pill
to swallow.

Because of the rejection,
Pauli didn't return to Durham,
to Aunt Pauline and Aunt Sallie.

Her heart was
broken.
Poetry
became her balm.
Therapy by typewriter.

John Brown's Body
by Stephen Vincent Benét
challenged Black writers
to speak for their own race.

And, again,
Pauli
couldn't keep her fingers still.

She dared!

She dared
to write Stephen Vincent Benét,
a famous author,
asking for an interview.

He wrote back,
asking for her work.

For years to come,
Stephen Vincent Benét would be
her critic
and her cheerleader.
Her guide.
His encouragement nourished the seeds of poetry
in her heart.

Writing poetry sustained Pauli's soul
while she tried to find
employment
to sustain her body.

After jumping from job to job
as work
materialized
and then
vanished,

Pauli found herself
unemployed.
Without the prospects
of graduate school,
she was forced
to apply for public assistance.
Welfare.

Sitting on hard benches at government offices,
waiting,
like cattle,
reduced to a number,
made Pauli's fingers burn again.

Around her, the faces of America,
dark and light,
immigrant and Indigenous,
pleaded for work.

Not for a handout.

But for work
so they could eat
and have a roof over their heads
and perhaps
a little
dignity.

    Why did it have to be that way?
    Freedom is a dream
    Haunting as amber wine
    Or worlds remembered out of time,

Not Eden's gate, but freedom
Lures us down a trail of skulls
Where men forever crush the dreamers—
Never the dream.[52]

Pauli's typewriter burned
at the shame
those sitting on the
long hard benches,
like she,
endured.
Things had to
change.

Confrontation by typewriter.
Again.

She wrote the *New York Herald Tribune*
and sent a copy
to Eleanor Roosevelt.

The First Lady
wrote about Pauli's experience
in her newspaper column.
She included an excerpt of her letter
not naming her,
but asking that her plight,
and that of the poor,
not be ignored.[53]

Although the First Lady
didn't totally agree,

she had listened.
And shouted Pauli's voice from a national pulpit.

Finally, Pauli landed a job organizing
National Sharecroppers Week.
She would be paid
for doing what she had wanted to do—
bringing attention to the oppressed,
both Black and white.
Bringing attention
to sharecropper families
indentured
to farmers who abused the absolute power they held
over
the sharecroppers' lives.

It was through this job Pauli finally spoke with
Eleanor Roosevelt.
In person.
This first encounter
marked the beginning of a
friendship
she never would have expected.

Pauli wrote Mrs. Roosevelt
in hopes
the First Lady would speak at the dinner
for the Sharecroppers Week
fundraising campaign.

Mrs. Roosevelt agreed
and invited Pauli and her colleagues

to her apartment
on Eleventh Street
in New York.

Mrs. Roosevelt won her over
with her grace and warmth.
At that first meeting,
already,
Pauli felt she'd found a kindred soul.
Another elderly aunt
whom she could trust
and love.
She found Mrs. Roosevelt to be
"utterly human."[54]

The First Lady agreed
to speak at the Sharecroppers Week dinner,
and award a prize for a children's essay contest.
Before Pauli left,
she handed Pauli a $100 check for
the cause.

Pauli was smitten,
but the young friendship,
which would eventually last a lifetime,
stumbled
immediately
on a racial incident.

A premiere of *Abe Lincoln in Illinois*
played in Washington, D.C.,
and the First Lady

crossed a picket line of Black protesters
not allowed at the theater
to watch a movie about their hero.[55]

Pauli's fingers flew.
Again.
How could the First Lady
not understand
the symbolism
of what she had done?
Crossing a picket line
of a protest
against discrimination
to see a movie?

The First Lady replied.
The premiere was funded
by a charitable organization
which
in her eyes
trumped
stepping over the rights of Black people.

Pauli didn't agree
but she didn't withdraw
from the friendship.

Her confrontations by typewriter
with Eleanor Roosevelt
creating a pattern.[56]

In a relationship
which was rocky at first,
Eleanor called Pauli a firebrand.
And Pauli always demanded
action
from the president.
To help her people.
To stop lynching.
To help the plight of Black servicemen.

As Pauli and Eleanor got to know each other,
respect grew.
Sometimes the First Lady was able to make changes
on her own.
Other times, she brought Pauli's pleas
before the president.

Pauli was invited to the White House often,
and to Val-Kill,
Eleanor's home in New York.
She was invited to intimate family gatherings
and when foreign dignitaries visited.
Their friendship perhaps strengthened
because both women's gender preference
went against the norms.

Pauli taught Eleanor Roosevelt
about what it was to
be Black.
Eleanor gave Pauli respect.
In the end, Pauli came to look at Eleanor
as a member of the family

who even visited in the hospital when she was sick.
It became a friendship of equals
despite the differences
in age,
social standing,
and race.

TAKING A STAND

Going home for Easter, in 1940,
Pauli and one of her housemates,
Adelene McBean,
rode a bus from New York
to Washington.

They planned to avoid
the Jim Crow laws
by driving Pauli's sister Mil's car
south
from Washington to Durham, North Carolina.
But Mil's car was in the shop.
A Jim Crow bus from Washington
was the only option.

How could she walk to the back of the bus
after the freedom
of New York?
How would Adelene?
She was from the West Indies.
She'd never been in the
South.

There's no way to keep your
dignity
walking through the cramped aisle,
between the
whites.
Everyone knows
you're in the back of the bus

because you are
inferior
unworthy
undeserving
of sitting with the rest.

Feelings she had avoided for years
came hurtling back,
but to top it all off, the last seat on the bus was
broken
and it hurt Adelene's back.

It seemed
reasonable
to move up a couple of seats.
Still behind the whites
but not in a broken seat.

And it could have gone without incident.
But sitting behind the whites
was not segregated enough
for the Virginia bus driver.

He stopped the bus
and tried to force the girls to sit in the very back
without fixing the seat.

Pauli Murray was a dormant volcano.
She had been preparing for this moment
all her life.

That day,

on a bus in Petersburg, Virginia,
she decided
she was a human being
like everyone else.

She had paid the same as the rest who rode that bus.
There was
no reason
she should have to sit
on a broken seat.
No one other than a person with
dark skin
would have been made to sit
on a broken seat
when other seats were available.

Pauli and Adelene refused.

They took a stand.

They knew they might end up in jail,
but what the bus driver asked was so petty
and insulting
and humiliating
that they couldn't let it go.

The confrontation escalated.
The police were called.
After several hours the seat was fixed
and the girls moved back,
as required.

But the bus didn't take off.

The humiliated driver had to have his say.
He handed out incident reports
to all whites
so they could recount what had happened.
He didn't hand reports
to any person of color.

When Pauli demanded
to have an incident report for herself,
and her friend,
she and Adelene
ended up in
jail.[57]

They shared a cell with three other women.
A cell with a toilet in the middle.
Without privacy from the other women
or the Black men
who filled the corridors in front of the cell
because there were not enough cells for Black men
while white men's cells stayed
vacant.
The men had a clear view
of everything
they
did.

The men heckled.

The women sneered.
What were uppity girls like Pauli and Adelene
doing in jail?

Always thinking,
her fingers always
burning,
Pauli had sneaked paper and pencil into her pocket
before they were booked.

She wrote the story of the arrest.
She wrote that she and Adelene
were fighting for the rights of people of color.

The letter got passed around
by the women
and to the men
and the others shared their own stories.
All of them
now
united.

Bedbugs
infested the mattresses
without sheets
in the cells
where they were jailed.
They had no towels, or soap,
yet
a sign on the cell directed the inmates to keep clean.

Impossible.

Pauli decided to challenge the prison system
of the Commonwealth of Virginia
because she had no way to follow its mandates.

She wrote the warden a letter asking for sheets,
and towels
and soap
and a mattress without bugs.[58]
Politely,
with reasons,
like Mahatma Gandhi,
a man from India
Pauli had read about
and who,
with "nonviolent resistance coupled with good will,"[59]
was demanding freedom
for India
from the British Empire.
Pauli admired him,
just as she later would admire
Martin Luther King Jr.
Because they both
advocated
change
through nonviolence.

She followed Gandhi's lead
But it didn't work.

The jailer did nothing.

Because they had been charged with breaking a
Jim Crow law,
the NAACP agreed to defend the girls.
The case, they hoped,
would make it to the Supreme Court
and set a precedent
by which
Jim Crow laws could start
toppling.

But the presiding judge knew there was no law
in Virginia
to make a person of color sit
in the back of the bus.
Instead,
they were convicted of
disturbing the peace,
which is what must have happened when they had the
audacity
to ask to be treated
like everyone else on the bus—
to have their side of the story
heard.

Their punishment was to pay
a $10 fine, and $11.70 for costs
of the trial—money
they did not have.
So back to jail they went
for several days
until the Worker's Defense League
paid what they owed.

This time
sheets covered their beds.
Towels and soap
were provided.
The cell was cleaned,
and the bedbugs cleared with acetylene torches,
which is what it took to kill what infected that jail.

Mahatma Gandhi's tactics worked.
The second time around.

It seemed like Pauli was doomed
to serve her sentence.
Her sister Mil
wrote Eleanor Roosevelt
asking the First Lady
to intercede
and get Pauli out of jail.

The First Lady
wrote
the governor of Virginia.
The Honorable Governor
believed the girls should have complied
with the law.
The First Lady
did not contradict him.

Eleanor Roosevelt,
even though she tried,
still did not understand

the humiliation
of being treated differently,
of being denied basic human rights,
of being considered to be
less than human.

In 1940,
going to jail
to demand civil rights
was not yet understood
or employed
in trying to force change.[60]

But it was coming.

In the end, the Workers Defense League
paid their fine.

Pauli's first act of defiance
did not make the national newspapers
like Rosa Parks
would
when she refused to give up her seat to a white man
in 1955.
But it was an important
formative
experience
for the activist in her.

She learned that her
words

and her pen
had power.

She learned that nonviolent resistance
worked.

She learned she had it in her
to rebel.

She had endured Jim Crow as a child.
She had run away from it to New York.
She had tried to heal its wounds.

Finally, she had begun to fight.

A SHARECROPPER'S LIFE IN THE BALANCE

A call for help
came
in 1940
from the Workers Defense League
to help workers who were oppressed
and sharecroppers who were cheated
or accused
of made up offenses
by the farmers
who owned or rented the lands they worked
for a share of the profits.

Sharecroppers Week earlier in the year
had been thirty-year-old Pauli's introduction
to the unfairness
and injustice
endured by families
whose lives were in the hands of farmers
struggling to put food on the table
for their own.

She could not refuse
the call
to fight.
It was time.
To be an activist.
For her people.
And for anyone,
Black or white,
who had been wronged through sharecropping.

The Workers Defense League gave her that chance.
And it became a paying job.

Raising money
for an appeal
of a murder conviction
was the job they offered.
The conviction
of a Black man who'd shot a white farmer
in self-defense.

Odell Waller,
a Black sharecropper
from Gretna, Virginia,
became her
cause.
A sharecropper
who refused to accept
injustice
and demanded what was rightly
his.

The county in Virginia
where Odell Waller farmed
was primarily farmed in shares.
There were landowners.
Then there were share-tenants and sharecroppers.
Share-tenants owned equipment,
but no land.
They paid the landowner in crops.
The sharecropper owned nothing.

Landowners and share-tenants paid sharecroppers
for their labor
in crops.[61]
Shares of crops.

The deal between twenty-three-year-old Odell
and Oscar Davis,
the share-tenant farmer
for whom Odell was a sharecropper,[62]
had been clear.
Odell was paid
one
out of every four bags of wheat he harvested.
Three
out of every six bundles of tobacco.
Three-fourths of the corn crop.

The deal was reached
the year before, in 1939,
when Odell Waller lost his home.
Odell's aunt, Annie Waller,
and her husband,
Willis,
had adopted Odell as a baby,
when Odell's father had died and his mother
couldn't support them.

The deal was reached
when Willis Waller died[63]
and Odell and Annie Waller
could not make enough money

and lost the land they had
owned.

The deal was reached for farming the land
and allowing Odell, his wife Mollie, and Annie
to live in a house on the property Davis farmed.

But times were tough.
The government cut back the amount of tobacco
farmers could grow.
Davis cut
the tobacco acres
that Odell farmed.
And Davis kept
all the government money.
Subsidy
meant to pay
for those two acres
that Odell had lost.

Without tobacco
and the government subsidy,
money was not enough to keep a family fed
and a roof over their heads.
Making ends meet
was impossible
for Odell
without another job.

After the crop was planted,
Odell

got a contract job in Maryland
laying electrical lines
so his family could eat.
Odell
paid his cousin, Robert Waller,
who owned a farm
and lived close by,
to help
Mollie and Annie
to work the land
and harvest the crop
so he would still be able to receive
what he was due.
Annie Waller
also took care of the sharecropper's sick wife
for a period of three weeks.

Bad faith was what they found
at the end of the harvest,
only three months after Odell had left.[64]
The white farmer didn't live up
to his side of the deal.

Oscar Davis refused
to give Annie Waller and Mollie
their share of the crops
and threatened to hurt Odell if he asked for it again.[65]

Minimum wage
in 1940
was thirty cents
an hour.

Thirty cents bought a gallon of milk.
Oscar Davis refused
to pay Annie Waller
the $2.50 per week
he'd promised her.
For taking care of his wife.
When Annie Waller asked for her due,
after three weeks without pay,
and when Annie Waller refused to farm tobacco
for which she knew she wouldn't be paid,[66]
the farmer
evicted them from the house they rented on his land.
The only shelter they could find was
a little cabin
lent by their pastor.
A man
who understood their plight.

Oscar Davis,
the white farmer
Odell and his family worked for,
was known to be a violent man
who carried a pistol
and wasn't afraid to use it.
Oscar Davis,
the white farmer
Odell and his family worked for,
had threatened
bodily harm
if Odell tried to press his claim.[67]

When a violent white man,

who carries a gun
in his pocket[68]
and often uses it
steals your share,
throws your family on the street,
refuses to pay your mother for weeks of work,
and threatens you with bodily harm,
it seemed smart for Odell Waller
to arm himself
before asking the man for his rightful share.

When Oscar Davis
refused to hand over what Odell was due
and reached inside his shirt,
Odell believed
the farmer was reaching for his
gun.

And Odell
defended himself.

The Constitution of the United States
guarantees
trial by jury.
Trial
by a jury of your peers.
But there was not a Black face,
or a brown face
or a poor face
on the jury
that tried Odell Waller.
Or one mind that could

understand
that refusing to pay for the care of
his own wife,
keeping his sharecropper's share
of the profits,
refusing to give his sharecropper even
a cent
of the government money that was due to him,
and leaving the sharecropper's family
without a home
was criminal.

There was not one face
or one mind
that could understand
 when a white man who always carried
a gun
and often used it
reached inside his shirt,
in an argument with a Black man,
whom he had already threatened,
the Black man would know for sure
the white man's intent
would be to kill.

Odell thought he was about to be shot.

Odell shot in self-defense.

Without a Black face on the jury that decided his fate,
Odell Waller
never had a chance.

To be included
in a jury
in the Commonwealth of Virginia
in 1940,
a person had to be a voter.

To vote
in the Commonwealth of Virginia in 1940,
a person had to pay
a poll tax
of $1.50
for three years in a row.

When a week's salary
for taking care of a sick woman
was $2.50,
it is easy to see
how
there were no Black faces on the jury
that would determine
Odell Waller's
guilt
or innocence.

So Odell was not tried
by a jury of his peers.
But by a jury of Oscar Davis's peers.
Ten of the twelve men
were farmers
with their own sharecroppers.
Ten farmers

who were just as strapped
as Oscar Davis.
Ten farmers
who may not have shared
their government subsidy
with their own sharecroppers,
either.
Ten farmers
who might have even refused
to pay their sharecroppers' share of the profits
because times were tough.

And Odell Waller did not have a good defense.
The Workers Defense League lawyer
scheduled
to defend him
was delayed at a Supreme Court hearing.
The lawyer's request for a continuance
of a few hours
was not granted
by the local white judge
who may not have seen the life of a Black man
worth the inconvenience
of juggling his court schedule.

The lawyer who ended up defending Odell Waller
was unprepared
and inexperienced
in matters affecting sharecroppers.
He was employed
by the Revolutionary Workers League
wrongly

rumored
to be
communist,
a kiss of death
in rural Virginia
even if Odell hadn't been Black.[69]

The jury that judged
Odell Waller
were brought up in a time and place
where having a dark face meant
being inferior,
irresponsible,
and often villainous.

> The drivers are dead now
> But the drivers have sons.
> The slaves are dead too
> But the slaves have sons,
> And when sons of drivers meet sons of slaves
> The hate, the old hate, keeps grinding on.[70]

They were brought up in a place
where a Black face was not coupled
with humanity
or the right to life.
They all believed Oscar's son
who said his father told him
on his dying bed
that Odell
had shot him twice
when he was down.

Two weeks before,
in his testimony
at the time of the shooting,
those words didn't come up
at all.

In a preliminary hearing,
they believed Oscar's wife when she said
that Oscar
didn't have a gun on him
even though no one else
could corroborate that fact.

They believed the only eyewitness—
a Black man who swore
that Oscar Davis
was kind and civil to Odell that day
even though Odell said the words Oscar called him
couldn't be said in public.

Two weeks was all it took to convict Odell Waller
of murder
even though the fact
that Oscar Davis
reached into his shirt
where he was known to carry a pistol[71]
pointed to self-defense.
Even though Oscar Davis
threatening
Odell
with bodily harm
if he asked for his share again

pointed to self-defense.
Even though when
Oscar Davis
refused to give
Odell
his rightful share
and left Odell's family
homeless,
he showed
what he thought
of the value
of Odell's life.
Odell was sentenced to die.[72]

The ten white farmers
along with a white businessman
and a white carpenter
gave a verdict of
guilty
to Odell Waller.

The job Pauli accepted was to try
to reverse his fate.
To raise $350
for an appeal.

Back to Virginia Pauli trekked.
To where, as a child,
a circle of white faces had surrounded her
at the train station.
To where she had so recently
been jailed.

To where she had sworn she wouldn't ride
public transportation
ever again.
To where
Jim Crow
still
reigned.

Back to Virginia,
the knowledge that Odell would die if she didn't succeed—
propelled her.

The shadow of Jim Crow had hovered
over Odell Waller's trial.
The shadow of Jim Crow still hounded Pauli.
Attempting
to raise funds in Richmond
with a white colleague,
Pauli and her friend had nowhere to stay.
Car trouble made them too late to find the lawyer
who was supposed to host them and
direct them
to lodging.
They had no way to find him.
A hotel would mean two rooms.
One in a hotel for whites.
One in a hotel for Blacks.
They didn't even have money for one room.
So Pauli reached out to her cousin
to lodge them that night,
but even her cousin
hesitated

to have a white woman
under her roof.

An appointment at a colored university,
Virginia Union,
to ask for funds at an assembly
was granted
when Pauli's articulate, unaccented voice
was mistaken
for a white voice
over the telephone.

But in person,
the color of her skin told the true tale
and she was prevented from speaking at the chapel service
to help Odell.

Black voices,
she was told,
did not impress as much as white.
Even at a colored university.

A conference of Black ministers gave her
dollars, and quarters and dimes,
all they could afford
to help defend their Black brother.
She raised $37.50.

The lie the witness told
was there for all to see.
He swore Oscar Davis

had been more than kind
to Odell
while they talked
about the crop shares,
and Odell shot him anyway.[73]
The injustice
of the poll tax
was there for all to see.
But that had all been ignored by the jury
and more than likely
it would be ignored on appeal.
There was nothing Pauli could do
but ask that Odell's life
be spared.

Yet she worked,
writing a pamphlet on his plight.
Crisscrossing the country
with Annie Waller.
Through the West.
Through the North.
Speaking in big cities and raising funds
for the appeal.

Through the campaign
Pauli not only raised funds
for Odell's appeal,
but she brought Odell's cause
and the plight of the sharecroppers
to the national stage.

In 1942, the appeals court
of the Commonwealth of Virginia
denied the pleading
that argued Odell was not judged
by a jury of his peers.

The Supreme Court refused to hear the case.

A desperate move.
Asking the president and Mrs. Roosevelt to intervene
on behalf of Odell
was the only chance.
And Pauli did.
And they responded.

Despite the president's letter,
the governor of Virginia would not see that the poll tax
meant the decision of the
life or death
of a Black man
was left in the hands
of white men
and only in the hands of white men.

With the governor's refusal
President Roosevelt
took himself
out of the picture.
FDR would not push the governor.
It was not his jurisdiction, he said.

When a group of activists,
including Pauli,
tried to see him at the eleventh hour,
he declined to intervene again.
It was not his jurisdiction,
he repeated.

An effort to picket the White House
was banned.
Picketing the White House in time of war was considered
unwise
and unpatriotic
even if the life of a man was in the balance.[74]

But Mrs. Roosevelt spoke up.
She advocated on Odell's behalf
right up until the hour of his execution
on the morning
of July 2, 1942.[75]

> Put it all down in a time capsule,
> Bury it deep in the soil of Virginia,
> Bury slave-song with the Constitution,
> Bury it in that vineyard of planters
> And poll-taxers, sharecroppers and Presidents.
> In coffin and outhouse all men are equal,
> And the same red earth is fed
> By the white bones of Tom Jefferson
> And the white bones of Nat Turner.[76]

There was nothing to be done other than

protest.
Pauli organized a march in New York
on behalf of the March on Washington Movement.

Five hundred marched.
Black and white.
To the beat of a muffled drum
to mourn Odell's death.
Carrying banners.
"Our dead shall not have died in vain." [77]

FINALLY, A DECISION

That summer, of 1941,
the lawyers took over Odell's case
and before the final push
to save him from
execution.
In the summer of 1942,
Pauli retired
to a camp in the Catskills.
Failed.
Confused.
Exhausted.

She gave lectures on sharecropping
to the Young People's Socialist League Summer Institute
in exchange for a cabin
without electricity
or running water
for most of the summer of 1941.
A place where she could write
and spend time with her friend
Adelene McBean
who was nearby.

And writing helped.
Encouragement from Stephen Vincent Benét
made her spirit soar.
Writing the story of her soul became her priority.
Proud Shoes,
the story of her family.

The story that she'd started for Miss Reigart
at Hunter College
so long ago
filled her life.

Until a letter from Howard Law School
made her reconsider.

Her work for Odell Waller had been noticed.
Leon Ransom,[78]
a recruiter for Howard University School of Law
thought she had what it took to be
a good lawyer.
In response to bantering
back and forth,
when she met him in Richmond,
Pauli had suggested he admit her and give her a scholarship
to the famous Black law school.
The letter came out of the blue.
Leon Ransom had agreed to her request.
He offered admission to Howard Law School
and a scholarship.

The conundrum was overpowering.
Writing or law school—
how could she choose between them?

But it wasn't as difficult
as she might have thought.
Back in New York,
from the Catskills,

Pauli had been staying at a white friend's apartment—
a friend who was on vacation.
Pauli was kicked out of the building
by the superintendent
because of the color of her skin.
He changed the locks,
and left her in the cold
without her clothes.

A doorman at another New York building asked her to
ride the service elevator
to attend a funeral gathering
for a white friend.

> "I felt as if the scab over a deep gash . . . had been
> suddenly torn off and the raw flesh underneath scraped
> against gravel." [79]

She couldn't avoid Jim Crow.
She couldn't run away from it.
She could try to repair the damage Jim Crow had caused,
but she would likely fail in the long run
because
the laws
were against her.

It would take
changing laws
to bring equality to
all.

If the laws remained the same,
writing her story
would help
NO ONE.

There was no choice.
The conundrum was over.
The law won.

part III

THE ACTIVIST IN TRAINING

HOWARD LAW

Howard Law School in Washington, D.C.,
was full of promise for Pauli,
the activist.
A school for Black people.
A prominent law school.
The front line of the fight
against Jim Crow.

Howard University students were humans
with dark skin.
Their backgrounds
different,
but their life experiences
similar.
They all saw life through the same darkened lens.
Segregation and discrimination,
prominent pages in each of their stories.
Their hearts cried like hers
at every injustice.
Howard offered a community that would prepare her
and would join her
in the fight to overturn Jim Crow.

Pauli managed life at Howard like she had at Hunter,
with help from a few friends
for shelter,
food,
and transportation.
All of which her scholarship
didn't cover.

Occasional checks from a person who'd supported
Odell Waller
helped her.

Cousin Susie Elliott, now a dean at Howard,
helped. Cousin Susie offered Pauli a home
of sorts
in the ladies' powder room
in a freshmen women's dorm.
It had a toilet, a sink, and access to showers.
With a cot, a trunk, a bookshelf, and a desk
next to a barely used sitting room,
Pauli's room was
a makeshift palace.

Quickly, Pauli's room became
a meeting place for undergraduates interested in
the fight.

And Caroline Ware
helped.
A white professor of law at Howard,
Ware was a brilliant woman who could not
teach lawyers at any white university
because of her
gender.

She became Pauli's mentor,
and her friend.
Skipper,
which is what Pauli called Ware,

rescued "Pixie"
often.

Skipper sent Pixie money
and coats and galoshes.
Took her along on her family's trips.
The Ware-Gardiner home in nearby Virginia
became Pauli's
second home.
The friendship lasted through Pauli's lifetime.
Caroline Ware became
her confidant,
her mentor,
her conscience.
She had Pauli's back
until the end.

By this time
Eleanor Roosevelt
fit firmly in Pauli's camp.
The friendship easy and deep.

What was it about Pauli
that pulled people to her side?
What was it about Pauli
that made them want to help her?

Pauli's vision was clear.
No human being
should be subordinate to another.
Not because of race.
Not because of gender.

Putting another human being in a subordinate position
was wrong,
wrong,
WRONG.

The toddler who would not accept one pancake
when she wanted three.
The girl who was called a child of destiny
by her pastor.
The young woman who refused to sit
in a broken seat in the back of the bus.
The advocate for Odell Waller
knew this.

And she planned to right the wrong.
Her certainty in her cause
so strong
she swept up others in her wake
like a tidal wave.

LEARNING THE LAW

At Howard,
Pauli learned about laws.
Laws that had freed her race
after the Emancipation Proclamation.
And the laws that had re-enslaved them
a few years later.
The laws they called
Jim Crow.

Lincoln's Emancipation Proclamation was only that—
a proclamation.
Not a law.

To end slavery,
amendments were required—
changes to the Constitution—
the fabric of our nation.
A fabric that unfortunately
failed to interweave
the rights
of those who were
Black and Indigenous.
Changes to which all future laws must conform.
The Thirteenth,
Fourteenth, and
Fifteenth Amendments,
all ratified by 1870 changed the Constitution
to carry out a new vision of freedom
for Black people.

Every law that came after them
must conform to those amendments.

The Thirteenth Amendment abolished slavery
and anything that made a person feel enslaved—
the "badges and incidents of slavery."

The Fifteenth Amendment guaranteed Black men,
but not women,[80]
the right to vote.
With other Black people voting,
Black men could run for office
and win.
With people of color elected
to the halls of Congress and state legislatures,
eventually Black people's needs could be
addressed.

Pauli's favorite amendment was the one in the middle.
The Fourteenth.
It banned unfair laws.
It guaranteed "equal protection of the laws."
It was meant to ensure each law treated each person
EQUALLY.
Even former slaves.

They were called the
Civil Rights Amendments.
And these amendments
opened the door to
equality.
The Civil Rights Amendments

put Black people on the same
footing as whites.
It was a bitter pill to swallow
for whites in the South.

And they didn't swallow it.

Instead, they passed laws to close
that door.
Towns and states in the South passed laws
to keep Black people
away
from white people.

To keep Black people as
"others."
Not worthy of the same rights.

To make the act of voting so difficult
and expensive
that Black people wouldn't vote.

Without Black people voting,
their rights would never be addressed.
They would continue
as "others."
Inferior others.
Forever.

Those were the goals of
Jim Crow laws.

Jim Crow laws
treated Black people as if they were still
enslaved.

At Howard Law School, Pauli learned that
if a law made by a town,
or a state,
or a municipality
does not conform to, or
violates,
the Constitution,
including its amendments,
it may be challenged in a court of law.

It takes a test case to overturn a law
that violates the
Constitution,
and it takes a very courageous person
to volunteer
as the plaintiff—
the person who claims to be injured—
for such a case.
It takes lawyers
and money
and months
and years
to prepare to fight the case as far as the
Supreme Court.
If needed.

And winning
wasn't guaranteed.

It took until 1896,
thirty-one years after the end of
the Civil War,
to find the perfect case—
Plessy v. Ferguson.

Homer Plessy,
a person only one-eighth Black,
sat in a white car on a train,
not in the car set aside for
Black people
as he was supposed to
in New Orleans
in the state of Louisiana.

Homer Plessy
refused to move when asked.

Unlike Pauli,
who in 1940
would refuse to sit in the back of the bus
without prior plan,
Plessy broke the law
in 1892.

On purpose.

He did it to *test* the law
and prove
that the Jim Crow laws that sent him to a separate car
were unconstitutional.

He and the NAACP hoped that if they proved
that law was unconstitutional,
it would show that
all Jim Crow laws were
unconstitutional.

In 1896, the Supreme Court wasn't ready
to be fair to Black people.
It wasn't ready for equality between
Blacks and whites.

The justices ruled that
so long as the car where Homer Plessy was supposed to sit
was equal to the car where whites sat,
the laws
could stand.

The Court called it
SEPARATE BUT EQUAL.

Plessy v. Ferguson
validated Jim Crow.
It did not overturn it.

When Homer Plessy
refused
to move to the luggage car,
he had hoped to change the fate
of every Black person in the United States
for the better.
Instead, it changed

for the worse.
The court had ruled that segregation was
legal.
And so segregation became
the law of the land.

Now
restaurants could refuse to serve Black people
as long as some other restaurant,
somewhere,
served them.
Or make Black people eat
at the back door,
while whites ate at tables.
Inside.

School systems could spend a fraction
of the money
spent on white children
to educate
the sons and daughters of people with
dark skin
as long as there were separate schools for Black children,
no matter how bad.

Pauli knew separate could never be
equal.
Knew it because she had lived it.
She'd used the out-of-date
and cast-off textbooks from white schools
throughout her education.
She'd had to relieve herself in the trees

because there were no bathrooms
that Black people
could use
along a road.
She'd gone to jail for refusing
to sit in the back of the bus.

When Pauli arrived at Howard,
the best and the brightest minds in Black law—
Thurgood Marshall,
Spottswood Robinson,
Leon Ransom—[81]
were already engaged in the battle
with Jim Crow.
They were working on overturning the injustices,
one case at a time.

Their goal was to prove
the differences in facilities
and the differences in services.
To prove that a Negro school
was not as good as a neighboring white school—
not equal.
A Negro hospital
was not equal
to a neighboring white hospital.
One community center
that served Black people
was not equal
to the community center that served whites.
They tried,
but they couldn't overturn Jim Crow

by concentrating
on buildings
and services,[82]
not on the fact that segregation was
inherently unfair.

Pauli knew that the humiliation of being treated
separately
was an injury
to a person with dark skin.
An injury
that had deep and long-lasting consequences.
She knew it
because she had experienced it.
She knew it
because she had seen others be subject to it.

She knew it was unfair.
She knew it made her and other Black people feel
inferior—
less than whites,
like slaves.
She knew in her gut
that regardless of what others thought,
Plessy v. Ferguson
had been decided wrong.

She knew in her gut
that Jim Crow laws were
unconstitutional.
But when she first entered Howard,
she didn't know enough

about the law to be able to argue
her point.

So she had to wait.
And learn.
And obtain a law degree.
All before she could fight it
on her own.

She had to wait
to fight it in the courts,
but she didn't have to wait to fight it
on the ground.
When Jim Crow came knocking,
Pauli dove headlong to answer the call.

TAKING THE REINS—PROTESTS

In 1943,
at a cafeteria near the university,
three Howard students ordered hot chocolate
and were not served.
They refused to leave
and the police were called.

The police ordered that they be served.
So they were served,
and they were overcharged.
When they instead paid the price listed on the menu,
they were arrested.

Students at the Howard campus were
enraged.
The administration counseled calm.
The students at Howard demanded redress.

The protest plan came from group sessions
in Pauli's powder room.
Women-led, because many men had left Howard
to fight in World War II.
Pauli held a workshop
to organize students
on activism—
knowing the laws,
applying pressure,
lobbying,
working
with community organizations.

Ruth Powell
was one of the students who was overcharged
for the hot chocolate.
For months before,
alone,
Powell had quietly asked for service
at Washington lunch counters.
When she was refused, she
sat
and stared
and waited
to be served.
Although unsuccessful,
Powell waged a quiet, one-woman crusade
against injustice.

Now Pauli, Ruth, and several Howard women[83]
organized other students
to protest
at the Little Palace Cafeteria
on U Street, NW,
near the university.

Pauli was the legal mind.

They decided to use Ruth's tactics and
the nonviolent means
of Mahatma Gandhi
Pauli had used in jail
in Petersburg, Virginia.

"Let us fight—but only when we must fight!"[84]

In small groups
at the cafeteria lunch counter,
Black students asked to be
served.
And were denied.
They sat quietly and read
or did homework
not raising a voice
or even an eyebrow.
Just as Pauli had instructed.

Pickets walked outside the restaurant[85]
with posters.
Amongst them was Pauli's friend
and teacher,
Caroline Ware.
On the third day, the cafeteria
gave in. They were served.

Pauli was ecstatic.
Nonviolent civil disobedience worked
once again.
They had waged a battle
and won.
They had proven
that acting with reason
and without violence,
they could
prevail.
It was another way to overturn
Jim Crow.

They tried again
in 1944
at the John R. Thompson Company,
a restaurant
in a white neighborhood close to
Capitol Hill.
A restaurant where thousands of Black government workers
could have eaten
after working hours
if only they would have been
served.

Again,
Pauli was the legal spokesperson
for the protest.
Each demonstrator signed a pledge
of good behavior,
nonviolence,
and utter silence.[86]

Picket lines marched
silently
on the sidewalk.[87]
White reporters queried
white patrons
and passersby.
The whites they spoke to overwhelmingly endorsed
serving Black people.

Six Black soldiers asked to be served,
and were refused.

They joined the protest.
A white lieutenant
asked the Black soldiers to leave
so that the Army wouldn't be
embarrassed
in case of an incident.

If the Army is embarrassed by
soldiers asking to be served at a neighborhood restaurant,
Pauli pointed out,
then all soldiers should leave.
The lieutenant cleared the restaurant
of servicemen.

Within four and a half hours, the Black students
were served.

Changing the world is
possible
when all it takes is touching
someone else's soul
and opening someone's mind
to the wrong they are inflicting.

But in 1944, Congress didn't want to change the world.
Congress threatened to cut off
federal funds
due to Howard University, if students didn't stop
the protests.
What was more important?
Integrating a few restaurants in Washington, D.C.,
or keeping open

a university to equip Black people with
the education they needed
to bring the monumental change
deserved by their race?

It's a question that shouldn't have
to be asked.[88]

Pauli felt betrayed by Howard's Law School faculty.
They had been sympathetic to their cause
yet voted to quiet the voices
calling for desegregation of cafeterias.
It was time to try
a different way.
And Pauli
had already been working on it.

FROM JIM CROW TO JANE CROW

At Howard Law School,
Pauli had hoped to find scholars,
both Black and white,
to guide her and be both
"intellectually stimulating and a powerful affirmation
of human dignity and equality."[89]
Howard Law would be a place
where she could grow.

But she met a stumbling block on the first day
of class.

Because she was a
woman,
she was the butt of a professor's
joke.

He didn't know why women came to law school,
he said.[90]
Obviously, women could never
practice law.
In that moment, he guaranteed
that Pauli would become the best student
in his class.

Men's louder voices
drowned hers during discussions.
More of a belief
of her male classmates and professors

that she had nothing of worth
to contribute,
rather than an oversight.

A notice
on the bulletin board inviting
"All male students in the First Year Class"
to a social function called
a smoker,
excluded her.

She marched
to Leon Ransom's office.
It was his
invitation
to the reception.
It had been his
invitation
that had brought her to
Howard.

"What about us women,"
is what Pauli said.[91]

Leon Ransom answered that:

> "The purpose of the smoker was [for the law firms] to
> look over first-year men for likely prospects. . . . Through
> their association with these experienced lawyers
> these young men would enhance their professional
> development."[92]

Apparently,
humans of the female gender didn't need
the connections
that male students made
at smokers,
where practicing lawyers and law firms
were invited.
There was no chance
women could get a job as
a lawyer.

Set up your own sorority is what Ransom
finally counseled.[93]

Only one other woman
attended Howard Law School that first semester.
That woman left,
and for the following three years, Pauli
was the only woman in her class.
There were fewer than four women
in the whole law school
for the four years Pauli attended.
Including her.

Why had Leon Ransom said
she'd make a fine lawyer?
Why had Leon Ransom offered
her a scholarship?
How could someone who had suffered
discrimination for the color of his

skin
discriminate
against her for her
gender?

"I'll show them,"
was Pauli's attitude.

Soon she had the best grades
in her law school class.

Sometimes
the discrimination was
subtle.
Pauli proposed a lawsuit
to fight segregation of all cafeterias
in Washington, D.C.

There was no law
in the nation's capital
to keep Black people
separate
from whites
in restaurants.

A long-ignored law actually mandated
desegregation.
Why shouldn't they try? The men
laughed.
Would they have laughed at her idea
if she'd been a man?

Years later,
the suit was eventually brought by another woman
and won.
Years of humiliation
might have been avoided
by Black people
in Washington, D.C.
if only
the men
had listened to Pauli.

Other times
the male students' discrimination against Pauli
was obvious.
And harmful.

The Chief Justice of the Court of Peers
was the highest honor a law student
could achieve.
Given
to the student with the best grades
at the end of the second year.
And only to that student.
Except this time that student was
a woman.
Pauli.
The first woman
to achieve that stature
and the Chief Justice of the Court of Peers seat
went empty
at the beginning of her senior year

because men in her class
refused
    to give
        a woman
            the honor.

Until she outshone them all
by such lengths
they had no choice but
to seat her.

THE IDEA THAT CHANGED THE WORLD

The more Pauli learned,
the more convinced she became that
Plessy v. Ferguson
had been decided
incorrectly.
That Jim Crow laws were
inherently
unconstitutional.

In her last year at Howard,
in a class discussion,
she let loose her
arguments.

> "The time had come to make a frontal assault on
> the constitutionality of segregation per se instead of
> continuing to acquiesce in the *Plessy* doctrine while
> nibbling away at its underpinnings on a case-by-
> case basis and having to show in each case that the
> facility in question was in fact unequal. In essence
> I was challenging the traditional NAACP tactic of
> concentrating on the *equal* side of the *Plessy* equation."[94]

She brought down the
house. But not the way she wanted.
Laughter
filled the room.
Again.

Including her professor,
Spottswood Robinson.

She might have erupted
like a volcano.
She might have been confident
and matter-of-fact.
She might have boiled inside
while ice dripped from her tongue.
She was, without a doubt,
sure of herself and her idea.

But it would take
research
and arguments
to prove her point.

It would take time.
Just like that first day at Howard
when the professor pushed her
to excel with his sexist comments,
the laughter in the room pushed Pauli
to prove them all
wrong.

For now, she made a
bet.
Ten dollars.
With Spottswood Robinson.
That *Plessy* would be overturned
in less than twenty-five years

on the basis of the Thirteenth
and Fourteenth Amendments.[95]

He took the bet,
but she knew he was still
laughing.

Her fingers
burned.

She decided to
prove her point
and argue her case
in her seminar paper.
She already knew the title:
"Should the *Civil Rights Cases* and
Plessy v. Ferguson Be Overruled?"[96]

And it would have been nice
to write the paper before graduation,
but she got an extension.
She postponed her
"I'll show you"
until the summer.
Because more pressing issues
took her time.

It was more pressing
to fight the Howard administration,
and ask
the administration

to fight Congress
for Howard's rights to funding
instead of allowing Congress
to quash Black voices
in protest.

And it was more pressing
to fight for her right
to admission
for a year of
graduate studies at Harvard Law School.

The reward for being first in class
at Howard Law
was the Rosenwald fellowship[97]
a grant for a master's degree,
normally taken at Harvard.

But Pauli was
rejected,
and the response to her application
was brutal.

> "Harvard Law School . . . is not open to women for
> registration. . . . Your picture . . . indicate[s] that you
> are not of the sex to be admitted to Harvard Law
> School. . . ."[98]

Like her friend
Caroline Ware,
granddaughter

of the first dean of the Harvard Divinity School,
Pauli was unable to attend Harvard because
she was a woman.

Acceptance to nearby Radcliffe
was offered
even though Radcliffe
did not offer courses in law
much less
a master's degree
in law.
Just one more sign that lawyers,
both Black and white,
thought women
unworthy
and incapable,
of carrying out the duties of their
lofty profession.

Pauli called it her "battle against 'Jane Crow.'"[99]
Trying to claim
her well-earned place
at Harvard.
She mustered all the resources
at her disposal. Even President Roosevelt,
an alum, wrote Harvard on her behalf.

Letters flew from her typewriter.
To the university.
To Harvard Corporation.
To the law school.
Her last-ditch effort cut deep:

"Gentlemen, I would gladly change my sex to meet your requirements but since the way to such change has not been revealed to me, I have no recourse but to appeal to you to change your minds on this subject. Are you to tell me that one is as difficult as the other?"[100]

It didn't work.

Like when the University of North Carolina
cited the state constitution
as the barrier to her admittance,
now,
Harvard faculty and administration
refused to shoulder the blame
for her rejection.
Instead, Harvard cited
World War II.
Most of the law school faculty were now
soldiers.

Having to fight these battles
and the constant pressure to prove herself
versus her male counterparts
had an unintended consequence.
Pauli became an unabashed
feminist.
The burr of gender discrimination would create a wound
that would fester
even as much as the wound of racism ever did.

She had been refused

the automatic acceptance
to Harvard—
a white university in Boston—
to sharpen the tools she'd forged at Howard,
which would let her fight Jim Crow
and get the credentials she would need
for a successful law career.

She was refused, but she still needed an avenue
to use her Rosenwald fellowship
for graduate work in law.
She had to find a school.
The perfect school.
One that accepted all kinds
of lawyers—including females and Negroes.
And one whose faculty had not been decimated
by the war.

Boalt Hall of Law in Berkeley, California,[101]
close to Los Angeles,
was that school for Pauli.
Tired of the overt
and subtle
segregation of the East Coast,
California and the West were appealing.[102]
Perhaps from there she could
launch her crusade against inequality
and find better success than what she could encounter
in the East.

Pauli wrangled a job as special correspondent
to *PM*,

a liberal newspaper.
They paid only for articles published, but still,
enough money for food and shelter
until her scholarship
to Boalt Hall kicked in.

Graduation from Howard was filled
with love.
Aunt Pauline and Uncle Lewis Murray
came to show their pride in her
accomplishments.
Mrs. Roosevelt invited Aunt Pauline
for tea.[103]
A large bouquet of roses arrived from
the president and the First Lady
on Pauli's graduation day.
She put it on the stage for all
to share.
But she kept a ribbon
from the bouquet
for herself.
Forever. [104]

Pauli Murray in the years
after graduation from
Howard Law School,
1945-1955.

Portrait of Pauli's cousin Suzie
Elliott, Dean of Women at
Howard University and one of
Pauli's mentors from a young
age. 1940-1944.

Portrait of Mrs. Pauline F.
Dame, 1950-1955.

Gardiner Means and Caroline Ware at
"The Farm" in Northern Virginia. Ware was a
teacher and a friend to Pauli from her time at
Howard until her death, 1980.

Thelma Stevens and Pauli Murray looking over States Laws, 1949.

Pauli Murray, with Sylvia Ravitch, Lloyd K. Garrison and Frank Horne on the date of publication of Proud Shoes.

LOC, LC-USZ62-12395

Harold P. Boulware, Thurgood Marshall, and Spottswood W. Robinson III confer at the Supreme Court prior to presenting arguments against segregation in schools during *Brown v. Board of Education* case. Spottswood Robinson was her professor at Howard, Pauli knew Marshall from her fight to enter the University of North Carolina, 1953.

March 23rd. 6th P.m.

Bus Driver... Adams

5 6

Position of Passengers in Bus.

Officers Sivings & Magee
Police Court March 28th 40

Defendants
Adelene mc Beant Pauli Murray.
Charge: Creating a Disturbance

Diagram of Bus   3/23/41
6:41 P.m.

Already showing signs of a legal mind, Pauli documented everything.
This is the bus layout which she drew to explain the situation
of the arrest in Petersburg, Virginia, in 1940.

Copy of Telegram

Please send collect!

3/24/40

To: Mrs. Pauline F. Dame
906 Cameron St.
Durham, N.C.

Easter greetings. Arrested Petersburg warrant
Greyhound Bus. Don't worry. Contact Walter White.

Pauli Murray

Sent by: Pauli Murray
Petersburg City Jail
Petersburg, Va.

Telegram Pauli Murray sent to Aunt Pauline when she was arrested
to let her know that she and Adelene would not be home for Easter.

part IV

ACTION

THE FORGOTTEN BET

The ten-dollar bet with Spottswood Robinson
might have been forgotten,
and writing her seminar paper challenging Jim Crow
might have become a chore.
But not for Pauli.
Especially not after the ride West
to attend Boalt Hall of Law
in California.
Her sister Mil, who was also heading
to Los Angeles for a new job,
joined her.

The ten-dollar bet was not forgotten
and writing her seminar paper did not become a chore
because the shadow of Jim Crow followed them
West.
Even in 1944.

Driving a car
bulging
with all their earthly possessions.
Riding on thinning tires.[105]
Little or no money in their pockets
and under war rationing.
Pauli and Mil drove for hours
each day
to avoid spending nights
in hotel rooms.

Busted tires and the physical demands of the trip

from Washington, D.C.,
to Los Angeles,
left the girls
exhausted,
as if having walked all the way.

But the physical demands of the trip were
nothing
compared to the
confrontations
with Jim Crow.

On the road,
motel owners denied them rooms
because of the color of their skin.
When they finally found a place open
to their race, dingy sheets and blankets
covered beds where bugs were more at home
than humans.

Finally at their destination,
a dilapidated building owned by
a Black Realtor and ready for condemnation
was the only shelter Pauli and her sister found to rent in Los
Angeles.
The only furniture,
one bed and a hot plate.
The place where Pauli would live
until the fall semester started.
But soon after they moved in, they found
a letter
posted on their door.

"The flat you now occupy . . . is restricted to the white
or Caucasian race only."[106]

In California?
The promised land?
Pauli investigated.
And she found whites in the area
had organized to drive out
Black owners
and residents.
She wrote about it for the *Sentinel*,
a Negro paper.
The *Sentinel* got protection for Pauli and Mil
from the police
and the FBI.
Black people organized to
fight back.
Pauli and Mil stayed in their meager home.[107]

In California, Pauli learned her blood
wasn't good enough. Literally.
Wanting to do her part, she answered a call
to donate her blood to help save soldiers
fighting in Europe and the Pacific
against the Axis powers.
But her blood, she found,
would be segregated
by the government.
Because Black blood was not good enough
for white servicemen.
Some white soldiers would actually rather
die

than have a Black person's blood
flowing through their veins.[108]

Each indignity was a knife that cut
into Pauli's heart.
Each form of discrimination she experienced
on her trip West made her more adamant than ever
to write her seminar paper.
The one that would show
Spottswood Robinson and all of Howard Law
the way to overturn
Plessy v. Ferguson
on the basis of violating
the Thirteenth and
Fourteenth Amendments
of the Constitution.
The paper she believed would topple
Jim Crow.

She spent countless hours at the law library.
She read
and read
and read.
And searched for the proof she knew
must exist, that separate
could never be equal.
First, Pauli found that the concept of race was defined
by men,[109] not nature.
In the United States, one drop of
Black blood made you a member
of the Black race.

In the writings of
Gunnar Myrdal,
Pauli found
sociological and psychological data
proving that Black people were not
biologically inferior to whites.
She found other proof from scientists that
segregation prevents children from learning
to the best of their abilities.

It was not broken-down schools
or tattered books
or underpaid teachers
that kept Black children from achieving
like whites.

It was not inferior ability.

It was the humiliation
and the degradation
of being separated and treated
differently. [110]

With that separation, those in
power handed down a verdict
to Black children that they were not
good enough.
That verdict set the course for the
rest of their lives.
The humiliation
affected each child's ability to learn.
Labeling someone inferior,

for whatever reason,
causes measurable damage
to that person. Even if they're white.[111]

"Should the *Civil Rights Cases* and
Plessy v. Ferguson Be Overruled?"
explained how Jim Crow laws
violated
the Thirteenth Amendment,
which not only abolished slavery but also
decided
that every human being had
the "right not to be set aside
or marked with a badge of
inferiority." [112]

By denying a person freedom
to do what they wanted to do,
to go where they wanted to go,
to live where they wanted to live,
to be taught with their white peers,
Jim Crow laws kept Negroes
enslaved.

By labeling Black people inferior, Jim Crow laws
set them aside. It caused
long-lasting effects.

Jim Crow laws
kept Black people apart
from white people,
and behind

white people.
Far behind white people.

The Fourteenth Amendment
enshrined the right of equal protection
of the laws.
But how could having to go outside a theater
to use the bathroom
when whites could use bathrooms
inside
provide equal protection?
How could being unable to occupy a room in a
"white" hotel provide equal protection?
How could having to pay a special tax
most Black people could not afford
or pass an arbitrary literacy test
to vote when white people
didn't have to
provide equal protection?

Being treated differently under any law
was against the Fourteenth Amendment.
And was,
therefore,
unconstitutional.

In her paper, Pauli concluded that
Plessy v. Ferguson
had been
unconstitutional
all along.
The Supreme Court decision,

which had confirmed Jim Crow laws,
was flawed.[113]

Pauli wrote that *Plessy v. Ferguson* must be overturned
to end Jim Crow. It had to be overturned
based on the violation of the Thirteenth
and Fourteenth Amendments.
Not on a case by case basis.

To overturn *Plessy v. Ferguson,*
lawyers should not try to prove the "equal" part
of the Plessy equation—
that buildings,
services, or
facilities
were not "equal."

But instead should concentrate on the humiliation
and degradation
inflicted by separateness,
which not only marked Negroes
with a badge
of inferiority
but also prevented them from taking advantage
of an education
and denied them progress
in the path of life.
No definition of equal had ever been provided,
but Pauli's paper showed that segregation—
separateness—
violated
both the Thirteenth and Fourteenth Amendments.

Separate
was not just
unequal
but also
unconstitutional.

All Jim Crow laws,
since they mandated segregation,
were
therefore
unconstitutional.

It was a conclusion that was
inevitable for Pauli Murray.
Fairness was woven into the fabric
of her life. It was what made her fingers burn
to try to effect change.
It had been forming since her mind
awakened. It was the fair share
of pancakes she sought from Aunt Pauline.
And the justice she wanted from
John Henry Corniggins's and her father's
murderers. It was the lack of fairness
she tried to avoid when she walked,
instead of riding on a trolley. Or drove herself,
instead of sitting on the back of the bus.
It was the fairness she sought when she fled the South
for New York. And the fairness she sought
when the bus driver in Petersburg refused
to hear her opinion.
It was the fairness she sought
from the University of North Carolina

and from Harvard.
And she wasn't alone. Every person of dark skin
sought the same fairness and justice
the Fourteenth Amendment guaranteed.

"EQUAL PROTECTION OF THE LAWS."

Pauli Murray mailed
"Should the *Civil Rights Cases* and
Plessy v. Ferguson Be Overruled?"
to Leon Ransom at Howard.
She didn't even keep
a copy.
She moved on. Her fingers burned
to address other issues of the time.
In the newspaper *PM*
and in the *Sentinel*, a Negro L.A. weekly,
she found
an audience.

ONE PERSON PLUS ONE TYPEWRITER

"One person plus one typewriter constitutes a movement,"
Pauli said.[114]

That summer of 1944,
waiting to enter graduate law school in Berkeley,
she wrote
for anyone who would publish her work
about Black people men who sacrificed
their lives
in Europe and Asia to fight against one race
persecuting another.
Yet, at home,
segregation still defined Black people as inferior
by law. Lynchings were still condoned.

Pauli's writing cried
for justice. Demanded
the right for those of her race to be treated
with the dignity they deserved—
as nothing less than
human.
Her fingers burned
on her typewriter.
Articles flowed.

She also wrote poetry,
recording the history of the Negro race
she had never learned
in school.

"Dark Testament"
is a poem
that sings
of what it is to be Black,
and tells the story
of the Negro people
from Africa to Pauli's day.
It appeared in print
in *South Today*
that Berkeley summer.

In "An American Credo,"
an essay,
she promised:

> "I intend to do my part [to fight segregation] through
> the power of persuasion and spiritual resistance, by the
> power of my pen and by inviting violence on my own
> body."[115]

Pauli's words rippled out
and resonated
in her readers' minds
causing changes.
Not changes in the laws of the land,
as she would have wanted,
but at least changes in the understanding
of her Black readers
that they were not alone.

> "Miss Murray a few days ago I found an old PM
> newspaper on the hiway [sic] dated August 20 with

your article facing me, so I read it. You are really on the ball, it is one of the best articles in [the] world for a Negro to read, you are right as can be in everything you say . . . . I'm in France, trying like everything to get back to the states, and I want to feel as an American and [be] treated like one, and it takes people like you, to see that it [is] done, if you only knew how much your article has built up my morale, it's 100% now (smile) . . . . Just a soldier named Chuck." [116]

Once enrolled at Boalt Hall,
Pauli's attention turned
to her new studies.
A different paper was required
and a different topic—
"The Right to Equal Opportunity in Employment."
She also had to pass the bar exam
in order to practice law.
But always,
whenever she found a willing ear
in the classroom
in her writings,
at cafes,
she discussed her idea of how Jim Crow
should be toppled.

AN ACTIVIST DRESSED IN LAWYER'S CLOTHES

Pauli was promised a job
at Howard University after graduation
from Boalt Hall.

Packed up and ready to move,
in 1946 Pauli was at the right place at the right time
when she was sworn in as an attorney in California
after passing the bar exam.
She met Robert Kenny,
the attorney general of California.
Robert Kenny
needed a deputy
and Pauli impressed him.
She decided to stay.
She was the first Black person to hold the job.

But the job didn't last.

Illness,
her own appendicitis
and her beloved Aunt Pauline's diabetes,
took her away from the job.
And the job didn't wait for her.
By the time she was able to return,
a soldier, home from the war, had claimed the job.

Pauli returned to Washington
both
to claim the job that had been promised
at Howard

and to watch over Aunt Pauline who
was in a Washington hospital.
At Howard Law, waiting
for Dean William Hastie to make good on his promise
of a job,
she helped in his defense
from charges of supporting communism.
The charges fell flat,
but so did Pauli's dream of teaching at Howard.
Dean Hastie left
to be governor of the Virgin Islands.
His successor did not recognize
the promise
Hastie had made.

Pauli returned to New York
and looked for work
wearing the one and only dress she owned—
black with white polka dots—to every interview.
She washed the dress
and hung it out to dry each night.

The jobs with the big law firms
went to those with degrees from
Harvard and Yale and
Columbia.
But mostly they went to men.
Not to women.
Definitely not to Black women.
Judge Dorothy Kenyon—who would later
become her colleague—told Pauli
women were "barely tolerated"

in the legal profession,
confirming
what Pauli already knew.

Having passed the bar in the state of California
did not entitle her to work as a lawyer
in the state of New York.
While she took that state's exam and waited
the required period before being sworn in,
she worked at the lowliest job in her profession.
She became a law clerk, earning $25 per week.
She had no authority or standing in the courthouse
even though she had a law degree.
But she did have a place to live—
an apartment she rented from her boss.

Even when she clerked for another lawyer
at $40 per week, Pauli was miserable.

As soon as she passed the New York bar exam
and was sworn in,
she accepted an offer
from a lawyer.
One who offered
to put her name on the office door
and pay her a commission
on the cases she tried.
In a trial in which she was defending
two prostitutes,
Pauli was mistakenly identified as
a defendant.
Of course,

the Black woman at the defense table had to be
a defendant.

For nine months she worked
and tried cases
without her name ever being put
on the office door
and accumulating a share of fees of at least $400,
which the lawyer never paid.

She was fortunate to meet Ruth Whitehead Whaley,
the first Black woman
to practice law in New York.
Pauli took over Whaley's clients
as the older woman wound down her practice.
Pauli set up an office in her home.

That home,
her apartment in Brooklyn,
had altered Pauli's family situation.
Aunt Pauline had come for Christmas
and stayed a month.
Six months later, she and Aunt Sallie
moved in
for good.
Although it was cramped with her law office,
Aunt Pauline,
and Aunt Sallie,
at least Pauli now had all her troubles
under her own roof.
Living just on the edge of poverty
even with their combined incomes.

When Thelma Stevens
of the Women's Division of Christian Service
of the Methodist Church
came calling in 1948,
it was a godsend.
The job Thelma Stevens offered Pauli,
researching Jim Crow laws,
provided an income.
A steady income,
which allowed Pauli to move her law practice to an office
outside her home
in 1949, while she did her research.

> "My clients were poor but they were satisfied clients, and
> they referred to me their friends who were also poor, so
> we all starved together!"[117]

But still,
the money from the Methodist women
added to her meager law earnings
and supplemented the income that supported
Pauli and her aunts.

The job Thelma Stevens and the Methodist women offered
was one for which she was uniquely prepared.[118]
The Methodist women
served the poor,
both Black and white,
in their settlement houses,
community centers,
and in their cafeterias and universities

across the country.[119]
But Jim Crow laws in the South
and segregationist customs everywhere
got in the way
of their charitable intentions.

The Methodist women
wanted to know
where Jim Crow laws
prevented them from serving
the dark-skinned poor
along with the whites.
And they wanted to know
where they only had to change
the minds and hearts of the neighbors,
but not the laws.

Pauli researched federal laws
and the laws
of every state,
every town,
every county,
and every municipality
in the country.
She researched
while working on her own cases
and even while she ran for city council
in Brooklyn.
At the end of the race,
she'd lost—
although not as badly as everyone expected.

It took two and a half years.
States' Laws on Race and Color
was published in 1951.
Consisting of a whopping 746 pages,[120]
it was much more than the Methodist women
ever envisioned.

The NAACP
bought copies
of *States' Laws on Race and Color*
for every member of the staff to use
in the legal attack against
"separate but equal."

Thurgood Marshall called it
"the bible."[121]

The American Civil Liberties Union
bought a copy for each state law library
in the United States.

A copy was even presented to
the United Nations.

Human rights agencies,
Black colleges and universities,
and selected law schools
all found the book
indispensable.

Before Pauli's book,
for each case,

lawyers would have to research
all the laws of a state or municipality.
But now,
with Pauli's book,
that knowledge was at their fingertips.
The lawyers could find
all the laws of each state and town
where a Jim Crow law was being challenged.
Now it was easy to see the extent
of the devastation
caused by segregation
and use it in their arguments.
With this "bible,"
more cases could be challenged.
More challenges could be won.

Pauli became known
and respected
by other attorneys,
by those fighting Jim Crow,
by those in government working with the laws.
She had made it easier to fight
the evil that had chased her since she was a child.
But still, the challenge to which she was
dedicated, overturning *Plessy v. Ferguson*
based on the Thirteenth and Fourteenth Amendments,
escaped her.

WHY ON EARTH DIDN'T YOU TELL ME?

After *States' Laws,*
Pauli sold publisher Harper & Brothers
the idea for another book.
The story that began as an essay
for Miss Reigart at Hunter College.
The story Stephen Vincent Benét
said she should write.
The story which had started
as a history
of her family's roots.
For her nieces and nephews.
And became a crusade
to right the wrong she experienced
when her teachers knew nothing
of the story and history of Americans with Black skin.
It would be the story of her people
and of her race.
Her family's saga.
She would call it
Proud Shoes, The Story of an American Family.
It was published in 1956.
Mrs. Roosevelt
reported it in her column as

> "American history which all American citizens should
> read. It will bring pride to our Negro citizens and
> greater understanding to all of us." [122]

Supported
by the advance money from Harper,

Pauli devoted herself to writing.
On May 17, 1954,
while Pauli researched *Proud Shoes*,
the world changed.
Brown v. Board of Education of Topeka
overturned *Plessy v. Ferguson*
on the basis of violating the
Fourteenth Amendment.

Pauli was overjoyed.
For every person of color,
the *Brown* decision finally brought
vindication
and affirmation
and an opening of doors
for those who followed.
At last, the law recognized
that people of dark skin were
wholly
human.
Equal.
Not inferior.
And must be treated
no different than any other person.
Pauli believed she now knew how thrilled
her grandfather must have felt
when the Emancipation Proclamation was signed
by Abraham Lincoln.
He was present at the first turning point
for their race. She was present at the second.
She could almost hear

the dominoes
of Jim Crow laws
falling.

> We have returned from a place beyond hope;
> We have returned from wastelands of despair;
> We have come to reclaim our heritage;
> We have come to redeem our honor![123]

In her elation,
Pauli noticed similarities
in what she read
about *Brown v. Board of Education*
with what she had written
that summer,
ten years before.
She noticed similarities
to a brief she'd written
for *Mendez v. Westminster*
when a school segregated students based
on their Hispanic last names
and nothing more than their Hispanic last names.
She noticed the similarities,
but she never imagined the truth.
In 1954,
when *Brown v. Board of Education* was decided.

When she collected the bet
from Spottswood Robinson in 1963,
she learned that Thurgood Marshall, Robinson,
and the NAACP

used her seminar paper
and her brief for *Mendez v. Westminster*
to win *Brown v. Board of Education*.
The idea he had laughed at
when Pauli presented it
at Howard
in 1944
was the idea which was actually used
in 1954
to desegregate schools in the United States
and begin the process
of dismantling
Jim Crow.[124]

"Spots, why on earth didn't you tell me?" was all that
Pauli could muster on that visit.[125]

Spottswood Robinson, her professor when she was
a student at Howard,
was part of the NAACP's team
to challenge
Plessy v. Ferguson.
During their preparations for Brown,
Robinson had remembered
Pauli's paper.
"Should the *Civil Rights Cases* and
Plessy v. Ferguson Be Overruled?"
Her paper was helpful in developing the arguments[126]
they had used.
Her paper was included in the *Brown* briefs—
the information handed to the Supreme Court[127]
stating why their arguments should prevail.

They had also used her brief for
the *Mendez* trial.
All proof that her argument was
correct.

Brown v. Board
was a landmark decision.
A decision which shook the foundations
of the modern world.
But no one outside that group
of male lawyers
for the NAACP
had any idea that Pauli's work
had been
pivotal.

"Why on earth didn't you tell me?"

part V

....

JANE CROW

CHANGE IN DIRECTION

It's undeniable
that around the time Pauli collected
her bet with Spottswood Robinson
she had already reached
a conclusion:
Being female might be as much of an obstacle
to success
as being Black.

By the time Pauli collected her bet in 1963,
she had become a successful lawyer.
She had a master's degree
from Boalt Hall, had been a member of
Paul, Weiss, Rifkind, Wharton & Garrison,
a prestigious white law firm;
she had helped the government of Ghana
codify its laws and was on her way to becoming the first
person of color
to obtain a doctorate in law
from Yale.

By the time Pauli collected her bet,
the civil rights movement
had begun.
Instead of isolated incidents like
Pauli and Adelene McBean
refusing to sit in the back of the bus in 1940,
and the two cafeteria protests
in Washington, D.C.
in 1943 and 1944. This was

a full-fledged movement.
Sparked
when Rosa Parks
refused to sit in the back of the bus in 1955.
Parks was called
"The Mother of the Civil Rights Movement."

The movement was necessary.
In the same way that towns and states worked around
the Emancipation Proclamation and the Civil Rights
Amendments
at the end of the nineteenth century,
many towns and states defied the mandate
to desegregate schools
handed down by *Brown v. Board of Education*.
They defied the mandate to dismantle Jim Crow laws
and customs
that was the corollary
to the landmark civil rights win.
The civil rights movement
took up the challenge to enforce that mandate
to obtain equal education,
equal employment opportunities,
and just plain equality
for people of color.

Parks's refusal to give up her seat
was followed
by Martin Luther King Jr.'s Montgomery Bus Boycott,
which organized Black people in Alabama
to provide transportation for each other
in protest of segregation of the bus system.

The Little Rock Nine
—nine high school students—
enrolled in a previously all-white
Little Rock Central High School,
in Arkansas,
in 1957.[128]
Students in 1960,
began a series of sit-ins at a Woolworth's lunch counter
in Greensboro, North Carolina[129]
demanding that Black people be served at any
and all
restaurants.
James Meredith applied and was accepted
at the University of Mississippi
just to have his acceptance
revoked
and the governor of Mississippi barring the door
when they found out that he was Black.[130]

They padlocked school doors, closed the gates to
knowledge,
Trafficked in calumny, spread evil rumors,

Like timber wolves stalking stray sheep,
Hunted us down, drove us from our homes, slew us.

Frenzied, they turned on their own God,
Dynamited His churches and temples!

Stampeded like fire-crazed wild herds;
Silenced voices of reason; trampled one another.

Frantic, they strove by harsh enactments,
Crafty delays, witless improvisations

To turn back our tides of inexorable insistence,
Hinder the oncoming flood of our destiny.

Victims of self-delusion,
Misread our calmness as acquiescence.[131]

FOR THE GALS WHO WILL COME AFTER

Pauli's activism had shifted
away
from civil rights.
The feminist burr on her side
was inflicting real pain.

Becoming a successful lawyer had cost her
dearly.
The amount of effort
required to find work,
the humiliation,
the poverty,
all because she was a woman in the legal profession
rankled.

Even though her legal experience and knowledge were
without question,
she had found entrance into the
fraternity of lawyers
difficult.

The dismissive attitude
of the Howard Law School faculty and her classmates in
1940
still prevailed.

But working for the firm,
of Paul, Weiss, Rifkind, Wharton & Garrison
had given her confidence.
It had

"earned [her] the right to be delivered from the civil rights struggle long enough to become a top notch lawyer. If I can do well here, it will mean much to those who come behind me, particularly the gals in the profession."[132]

So she turned the page
from the fight against Jim Crow
to the fight against Jane Crow.
She moved seamlessly from one to the other because
gender and race
were a continuum
that she traveled.
An in-between from which she understood
the many sides.
She was a peg
that did not fit
into any holes.
She was a bridge between them.

She didn't abandon civil rights. Her focus just
shifted.
The change was made easy because
the civil rights movement
was still a man's movement.

Just like no man had thought Pauli should get
credit
for the idea that won
Brown v. Board of Education.
Or even tell her that her papers
had been used.

Women were allowed as
girlfriends,
and typists
and copy makers.
Phone-calling machines.
Organizers.
Coffee makers.
Not decision-makers.
Not drivers of policy.

Discrimination is an affront so deeply felt,
anyone who has suffered it
should never, ever inflict the same
on others.
But the male leaders
of the 1963 March on Washington for Jobs and Freedom
did just that.
Relegated women
to the back of the bus.
One lonely woman delegate
met with President Kennedy
after much adverse publicity.
No woman spoke that day
to the masses assembled.[133]
No woman even neared
Dr. Martin Luther King Jr.
Rosa Parks
was asked to walk with the wives.[134]
Why, Pauli asked again,
would Black women
subordinate

their quest for equal rights
to the male's quest?
Why couldn't they both march
in unison?

Pauli realized
that because the leaders
of the civil rights movement
were men,
they would not place enough value
on her
and her work.
It would be a struggle.
She still wouldn't get credit.
Even though getting credit was not her goal,
she knew
whatever change she could make happen
for people of color,
would affect less than a third of the population.
If she tried to end
discrimination against women,
more than half of the population would benefit,
including her Black sisters,
those who needed her help the most.

IT HAD HAPPENED BEFORE

It had happened before.
It had happened to Elizabeth Cady Stanton
and Lucretia Mott
when they were prevented from speaking
at the World Anti-Slavery Convention
because they were women.
Women
working for the rights of Black people
in the nineteenth century who realized that they,
themselves, had no rights.
No right to education.
No right to vote.
No right to inherit.
No right to keep any money earned.
No way to get out of a marriage
no matter how bad
because they were allowed no money
of their own.
It was abolition
that led women in the nineteenth century to
demand the vote.

They did not get it
until 1920.

But it took more
than getting the vote.
Actually, the vote made
little difference.

Women
still marked their ballots
the same way their husbands did.
Very few graced the halls of Congress
as representatives
or senators.
Without numbers of women in Congress,
no changes could be made
to the laws
that held women
down.

Most colleges and universities
still denied
women
acceptance to lofty professions
like medicine,
or law,
or engineering.
Banks denied them credit
to buy cars
or homes
without the signature of a man.

At the end of World War II,
women were asked to leave
lucrative jobs,
important jobs
they'd performed during the war,
for the returning soldiers.
The tank,

plane,
and munitions factories
turned to peacetime use,
and began to produce appliances
large and small.
The allure of the electric vacuum cleaner
and the washing machine
was touted over the airwaves.
A siren call
to women
to stay home and perpetuating the myth
that women
couldn't
shouldn't
wouldn't
be happy working outside the home.[135]

A myth
that also blamed
working women
for juvenile delinquency
and cowardice in soldiers
even though the first had no basis in fact
and there had not been enough women in the workforce
before the war
for the latter
to have been true.

But making lunches and
washing
and vacuuming

were not enough for many women.
They were bored,
unhappy.
Told by their doctors they were mentally
unbalanced
because they were unhappy.

But women knew they were not
mentally unbalanced
and women wanted more than
washing clothes
and doing dishes.
And many women,
both Black and white
working to obtain civil rights for Black people,
realized
again
that they were fighting for rights
they, themselves,
did not have.

Betty Friedan,
a journalist and mother,
wrote about it.
Her book,
The Feminine Mystique,
debunked the myth
that women were happy being
wives and mothers.
And nothing else.
A life of endless peanut butter sandwiches

and striving for the whitest of whites
in the daily laundry
wasn't fulfilling.
Even if they got to dance
with the vacuum cleaner.[136]

In 1963, *The Feminine Mystique*
became the women's bible.

THE WOMEN'S MOVEMENT

Pauli had been called
from Paul, Weiss, Rifkind, Wharton & Garrison
to teach in Ghana
to help codify
the laws
of the emerging democracy.

While in Ghana,
Pauli impressed a professor,
this time from Yale University,
and obtained admission and a fellowship
to earn a doctorate
in juridical science
at the Yale Law School.

Her official involvement with what became
the women's movement
began while she was at Yale.

While she was a doctoral student,
the President's Commission on the Status of Women
was formed by President John F. Kennedy
in 1961. Eleanor Roosevelt headed it.
Caroline Ware was a commissioner.
Pauli served on the Committee
on Civil and Political Rights.

One goal of the commission was to move women

"toward full partnership, creative use of skills, and genuine equality of opportunity."[137]

Another was to decide whether the president should support
the Equal Rights Amendment.
Pauli's job would be
writing something akin to
States' Laws on Race and Color.
This time, she would be writing
for gender discrimination.

Pauli was exceptionally qualified for the job
of examining laws that discriminated
against women
strictly on the basis of sex.
Laws that denied women
equal protection.
Laws that violated
the Fourteenth Amendment.

Jane Crow!

It was a bittersweet time
and a momentous accomplishment.
But before the work was done,
Pauli lost a dear friend
and a most ardent champion.
Eleanor Roosevelt
died.[138]
Pauli was bereft. Eleanor Roosevelt had been
a sister at arms,
a confidant,

a cheerleader,
a mother, and an aunt all rolled into one.

The report of the Commission on the Status of Women
was given to President Kennedy
on October 11, 1963.
The anniversary of Mrs. Roosevelt's birthday
and six weeks before
Lee Harvey Oswald
took John Kennedy's life.

The report of the commission was consequential,
but more consequential was the network
of women that formed
as a result.
Capable,
intelligent women
who had achieved success
in government,
as lawyers,
journalists,
writers,
defying odds.
Women who wanted
equality
and respect.
And the same educational and job opportunities
as their male counterparts.
Women who wanted to lay down
the groundwork for those who would come
after them.
Their names seldom appeared in newspaper headlines,

yet
they were on a sacred mission:
recognition of women's worth as human beings.
Nothing more
but nothing less.

Pauli was at the apex
of that network. Her typewriter
overflowing with letters
whenever her fingers burned.
She kept the coalition together,
taking advantage of every opportunity
and birthing the movement.

The most important opportunity came
with the Civil Rights Act of 1964.
The legislation meant to
guarantee
equality in the workplace.
Legislation intended to bar discrimination in employment
on the basis of race,
creed,
color,
or national origin.

Equal pay
for equal work.

But as the act was headed for a vote,
Howard Smith,
a representative from Virginia,
added a fatal amendment.

Some said it was
a joke.
Others said it was
intentional sabotage.
Howard Smith added "sex" to Title VII of the act,
the section speaking to bases
of forbidden discrimination.

Howard Smith was convinced
no member of Congress would vote for the act
if it gave women the same rights
for pay
and employment opportunities
as men.
In his opinion,
women were not intelligent,
or capable of rational thought.
And really,
they didn't need to work.
Men would take care of them.

Smith knew he was not alone
in his thinking. He counted on the threat
of equal pay and employment opportunities
for women
to defeat the bill.
The bill whose purpose was to recognize
Black men[139]
as equal to white men in the workplace.
Smith wanted to stop that change. Because he didn't think
Black men deserved equality in the workplace.

He wanted to allow his constituents
in Virginia
to continue discriminating against Black people
in the workplace.

Smith was right,
in a way.
Advocates for civil rights in Congress
were afraid
that adding equal rights for women in employment
would defeat the act.
And the act must be passed to guarantee Black men
equal rights in the workplace.
A righteous goal in everyone's minds.

They tried to remove Smith's "sex" amendment,
but they didn't count on the network of women who had
coalesced
as a result of the President's Commission.

They didn't count on Pauli's network,
or on Pauli's flying fingers.

> "A strong argument can be made for the proposition that
> Title VII without the 'sex' amendment would benefit
> Negro males primarily and thus offer genuine equality
> of opportunity to only *half* of the potential Negro work
> force."[140]

That's what Pauli wrote
on a paper that went to senators
and to Vice-President Hubert Humphrey,

and to Attorney General Robert Kennedy.
She sent it to Lady Bird Johnson,
the wife
of President Lyndon Johnson,
just like so many years before,
she had sent messages for President Roosevelt
to Eleanor.

The First Lady responded—
the president supported the bill in its present form,
guaranteeing equal opportunity
for both Black people and women
in employment.

Martha Griffiths
one of twelve women
in the House of Representatives,
and Margaret Chase Smith
one of two women in the Senate
used Pauli's arguments to push the bill
through.
Another epic win.
And this time, thanks to Pauli
and the network,
women were
included.

Title VII of the 1964 Civil Rights Act
can be considered
the single most transformative legislation
for advancing women's rights.
It allowed women to pursue

any job
for which they were qualified.
It ensured equal pay
for equal work.
For the first time,
a man and a woman doing the same job
would have to earn the same.

With higher paying jobs and
equal access to education,
women could earn more money.
With the recognition of women's abilities,
women could climb corporate ladders
and earn higher salaries.
In some cases, the higher salaries would bring
luxury.
In most cases, the higher salaries would help bring women
and their families
out of poverty.
Many of the injustices Pauli had suffered
in the workplace
could have been avoided
if only Black lives
and women
had been considered in earlier legislation.

IT TOOK MORE THAN THE
CIVIL RIGHTS ACT OF 1964

Pauli finished her work at Yale
in 1965, at age fifty-five,
not long after the act was passed.
Her commencement at Yale Law School
was ripe
with firsts.
For her family, she was the first to earn
a doctorate. She was the first to
graduate from a major university.
For Yale,
she was the first Black person
to attain a doctorate in juridical science.

A doctorate from Yale
did not put bread
on the table, and once again
Pauli was unemployed
with no reliable means
of support.
But Pauli was not idle. She sustained herself
by writing and speaking.
She concentrated her energies in cementing
women's newly won gains.

There should have been no question,
that the 1964 Civil Rights Act
would benefit women. But
the Equal Employment Opportunity Commission (EEOC),
the agency created to

enforce the act, treated equal employment opportunity
for women
as a joke.

Just like Howard Smith
of Virginia.

"Help Wanted, Male" and
"Help Wanted, Female"
want ads were still permitted.
Which allowed employers to limit
the pool of candidates for higher paying jobs
to only men.

Complaints
of race discrimination
were processed.
Complaints
of gender discrimination
were not.

The commission reported great progress when,
in truth,
there was little.

As vital as eliminating race discrimination
in the workplace was, Pauli thought,
a rising tide should lift
all boats.
Women could not be
left behind.
It became clear to Pauli

that an association like the NAACP,
with the purpose of fighting
for women's rights
and holding onto the ground
already hard fought for and gained,
was absolutely necessary.

NATIONAL ORGANIZATION FOR WOMEN

Once again,
Pauli's fingers burned
on the typewriter.
This time, to the coalition of women
in Washington. Mary Eastwood and she coauthored
"Jane Crow and the Law:
Sex Discrimination and Title VII,"
arguing that race
and gender discrimination
were two sides
of the same coin.
It was published in the
George Washington Law Review.

She fought.
Against the Equal Employment Opportunity Commission.
Which was not protecting women
from discrimination in the workplace.

In a speech before the National Council of Women
Pauli proposed that
if Title VII of the Civil Rights Act
was enforced by the EEOC,
women would have the opportunity
to advance
in the workplace
according to their abilities,
the
    same

as
      men.

Unfortunately,
the EEOC did not enforce the law
when it came to women's
grievances in the workplace.
And there was no organization,
no political power,
at the time,
that would do so.

Women must organize,
Pauli said in that speech.
Another march on Washington
should not be needed,
but if necessary,
"I hope women will not flinch from the thought."[141]

A *New York Times* article
quoting the speech
stated,
incorrectly,
that Pauli proposed
a protest
for women's rights.

Betty Friedan,
who was still involved in overturning
the feminine mystique,
gave Pauli a call.

If Pauli was proposing a protest
for women's rights,
Betty wanted to be in on the ground floor.

Betty Friedan became
Pauli's friend.
Easy.
Because both women
saw gender discrimination
with uncommon clarity.
Pauli introduced her to
the loose coalition of women
from President Kennedy's Commission—
her army.
Friedan called the group

   "the underground network of women in Washington."[142]

Like Pauli
and the underground network,
Betty Friedan wanted to preserve and exercise
the gains
in employment law
they had worked
so hard
to secure.

It became clear that
an organization to advocate for women's rights
could not wait.
But still they tried,
at first,

to work within the contours of the law.

Many of the women in the underground network
met at the Third National Conference of State Commissions
on the Status of Women.
A conference where the gains
in women's rights were to be discussed.

Some, like Pauli,
were commissioners.

They wrote a resolution
to require the EEOC to enforce the law
in cases of gender discrimination

They were
overruled.
They weren't even able to bring the resolution up
for a vote.

That day at lunch,
led by Betty Friedan,
twenty-eight women
each put up $5
to form
the National Organization for Women (NOW)
Their mission:

> "To take the actions needed to bring women into the
> mainstream of American society *now* . . . in fully equal
> partnership with men."[143]

Pauli became a founder
and a member of the organizing committee
along with Friedan
and Caroline Ware.

NOW
defended women
who suffered workplace discrimination.
Just like the NAACP
defended Negroes
against Jim Crow laws.

A female lawyer carried a piece of
telephone equipment
during her statement to the jury to show that
when Southern Bell Telephone and Telegraph
Company denied Lorena Weeks
the right to a high paying job because women are
inherently weak,
they were
wrong.[144]

NOW
stopped the practice of separate help wanted ads
for males and females.

NOW
advocated for equal pay for equal work
for women as well as for equal opportunities
in education.

NOW

prevented the rights and opportunities gained
by Title VII of the 1964 Civil Rights Act
from evaporating.

At the same time she volunteered for NOW,
Pauli continued her fight.
This time, she was again fighting
at the intersection
of race and gender—
with the American Civil Liberties Union, ACLU.

White v. Crook was the landmark case
against excluding
Black men,
and women, both Black and white,
from serving on juries.
Judge Dorothy Kenyon and Pauli
wrote the brief
basing the argument on the Fourteenth Amendment,
"Equal Protection of the Laws."

The victory they earned
turned the tide of discrimination
in the courts.

From now on,
Black faces
and female faces
would be seen in jury boxes.

Had Odell Waller
been tried after their victory,

the outcome might have been
different.

Ruth Bader Ginsburg,
who later became a Supreme Court Justice,
used Judge Kenyon and Pauli's strategy
in her own Supreme Court victory
in *Reed v. Reed,*
the first law on gender discrimination to be struck down
on the basis of Equal Protection.
Unlike the men who won
Brown v. Board of Education of Topeka, Kansas,
Ginsburg
credited Pauli and Kenyon
for her win.

A MAN TRAPPED IN A WOMAN'S BODY

Pauli Murray
had felt
all the indignities
of discrimination.

A Black woman
with white
blood
in her veins.
A woman
who at every turn
wondered
how her life would have been
had she been a man.

Even Aunt Pauline
knew Pauli
had a "boy/girl thing."

To Pauli, gender
was more than a hindrance.
She always wondered,
even when young,
if she was a man trapped in a woman's body.

Transgender
is possibly
what Pauli would call herself
had she lived in the twenty-first century.

Pauli's pronouns may have been
they/them/their.

In her quest to understand herself
she collected clippings
and tried to talk doctors into giving her
hormone therapies,
which were just beginning to be used at the time.
She even had a doctor try to find
hidden male organs
inside her body
during an appendectomy—
in the hopes of finding out
if she had male organs
hidden within her body—a condition known as being
a hermaphrodite.

Hospital stays for her were common
from overwork and stress,
but perhaps it was the effort
to fit in ways she could not
that strained her health
and emotions
to the breaking point.
Malnutrition and bad living conditions
made her physically sick.
Knowing that she loved women—
a love that was forbidden—
was enough to make a person's emotions strain.
Coupling the emotional strain
with the tendency
of doctors

at that time
to deem women hysterical
by nature
and emotionally unbalanced,
it is not surprising that Pauli spent time in the hospital.

Pauli was attracted to women,
particularly white women,
not to men.

Since childhood,
she had liked
the clothing of men and boys,
asking her Aunt Pauline
to buy her boy's clothes,
wearing her scout outfit
while traveling across the country
with Peg Holmes.
Men's clothes to her were just
plain comfortable.

In her relationship
with Peg Holmes at Camp Tera,
during the Great Depression,
she had been open with Peg about her love
and Peg had returned those feelings,[145]
although, in the end, it did not work out.

There may have been other relationships.
At the law firm of
Paul, Weiss, Rifkind, Wharton & Garrison,
Pauli met the love of her life,

Renee Barlow.
"The chemistry of our friendship produced sparks of
sheer joy."[146]
They never lived together
other than for joint travels.
Their relationship lasted until
Renee died in 1973.

Although Pauli alluded to deep relationships
with several women,
and she did act, on her relationships with Holmes
and with Barlow,
Pauli never came out as lesbian,
not even in her autobiography,
Song in a Weary Throat.
She skirted the issue.
Defining her relationships as friendships.
It's only from her personal letters that the truth emerges
and sometimes they're not even definitive.

It's possible she never used the word "homosexual"
because homosexuality,
at that time,
was considered a mental illness
and there was nothing sick
about the way she felt.

And homosexuality was dangerous.
In the 1950s,
McCarthyism
considered homosexuals
a threat

to national security
with the possibility
of making obtaining
a job
even more impossible
for someone like Pauli.

She had no leeway
to act out
her gender preference
or sexuality.
But she expressed it
as best she could.
Not openly
but reveling
in the moments
life gave her
with Renee.
Unobserved
and unfettered.
Their letters the only witnesses
to their everlasting love.

Pauli fought for human rights.
It was
a beginning
and an opening.
Giving each human worth,
whether Black or white,
male or female,
meant starting the discourse toward understanding.
But Pauli Murray did more than fight.

"The armful" Pauli Murray
carrying Peggie Holmes,
Pauli's first relationship, 1937

Pauli & Peggie in an acrobatic
stunt - Peggie balancing Pauli
in the air, 1937.

Pauli catching the old freight,
New York City. Pauli hopped
on trains like a vagabond to
return form California to
North Carolina because Aunt
Pauline was sick, 1935-1938.

Pauli in her scout uniform.
This was the picture she
chose to use in *Negro Anthology*
along with her essay "Three
Thousand Miles On a Dime
in Ten Days." She called
herself "Pete" in that
essay, 1931.

More of same . . . "The
Dude" - 1931. Pauli Murray
seated on a stone wall.

Irene Barlow wearing a
bathing suit standing on the
sand, 1932-1939.

Pauli - Writing a poem on
Riverside Drive. Election
Day, Nov. 8, 1938 - N.Y.C.

Portrait of Irene Barlow in
later life. Irene was the love
of Pauli's life. She cared for
Irene until Irene's death,
1965-1972.

She ensconced the laws
that would make it possible
for each human's rights to flourish
so that someday
some little girl
who wanted to wear boy's clothes
could do just that.
So that everyone would someday be free
to love
whomever they wished to love
without persecution
and to live life
as their true selves
without fear.
She broke down the barriers
and built the ladders
so that others could climb.
Not just toward equality,
but toward their own kind of happiness.
Whatever that may be.

She strove
to make a difference
for those who couldn't advocate
for themselves.

part VI

THE LEGACY OF ACTIVISM

AN UNSUNG FORCE

Pauli's work was pivotal in the fight
against Jim Crow

In the women's movement, Pauli was
a leader.
A mover.
A recognized force.

She was an
activist. That's what she was born
to be. She fought discrimination
against race and against gender,
long before there were
nationwide movements.

Her words rippled out
from her burning fingers
to a typewriter
and made change happen.

Her words also recorded
the history of her family
and through it,
the history of the Black race.

Her words made poetry that soothed the soul
and fired up the mind.

After her work with women's rights,
she taught.

Men and women not only received
an uncommon understanding of the law
but also a deeper understanding of
race and gender.
Of fairness
and equal protection.

At Benedict College, she worked
to close the gap in education between
Black and white students.

At Brandeis University, she created
and taught an Afro-American Studies program.

But she was out of step
with the activism of the Black youth of the 1960s.
The women's movement didn't address
the poverty, lack of education,
and unemployment
of her Black sisters.

After her beloved Renee died in 1973,
Pauli gave it all up to
minister to those in need by becoming
an Episcopal priest.

The Episcopal faith had been a pillar
of Pauli's life,
starting with reading the Bible
to her granma Cornelia
who had been baptized in the Chapel of the Cross
in Chapel Hill, North Carolina.

Aunt Pauline and Aunt Sallie
were behind the founding
of St. Titus Church—
the tiny Episcopal parish church
in the Bottoms—
devotion to their church central to their existence.[147]
St. Titus rectory became Pauli's second home
when Aunt Sallie married
the Reverend John Small.
Later, spending summers helping her aunt and uncle
when they moved to Croom, Maryland,
to a bigger parish.
Throughout her life,
she had practiced her faith
and lived by it
without fail.

On October 25, 1955,
just a month after Aunt Pauline
had turned eighty-five,
it became obvious that
her mother
would not last the night.
Pauli tried to find
a priest.
But a priest could not be found.
And Pauli read the prayers,
the Psalms and the prayers
to ease her mother on
to the next life.

Her faith was her bond to her dear Renee,
both committed
Episcopalians
and again
at the time of Renee's death
Pauli read the prayers,
the Psalms and the prayers
to ease her love on
to the next life.

And she ministered
to her
and her family
after Renee's death.
For the second time,
without ordination,
she had acted like a priest.

With Renee's death,
Pauli faced her own mortality
and knew
from that point on
her mission on earth
would revolve around the church.

She studied
for the priesthood
when women had little hope
of becoming a priest.
But ending up
in 1977

in the first group
of women
to be ordained.

She held her first service
at the Chapel of the Cross in Chapel Hill,
North Carolina.
The chapel where
her grandmother, a slave,
had been baptized.
She spoke behind the lectern
bearing the name of her great-grandaunt—
Mary Ruffin Smith—a white aristocrat.
She used her slave grandmother's Bible
and marked the readings with a ribbon
from the bouquet Eleanor and Franklin Roosevelt
sent her when she graduated
from law school.

A HUMAN OF WORTH

Pauli Murray
died on July 1, 1985.
A year before Halley's Comet
returned,
a few months short of reaching
seventy-five.

It was her idea
that sparked the defeat of the laws
that discriminated against Black people.
It was her work
that gave a legal basis to
the women's movement.
While she was alive,
she was an unsung force.
Now we know she was
transformative.

Pauli Murray, a faculty
member at Brandeis, standing
with Coretta Scott King on
the occasion of the Brandeis
commencement, 1969.

Pauli Murray standing with
Eleanor Roosevelt at Valkill
Cottage, Hyde Park, New
York. Pauli was often a guest
there and at the First Lady's
New York apartment, 1962.

Group portrait of NOW
founders at the Third
National Conference of State
Commissions on the Status
of Women where NOW was
formed in 1966.

Pauli Murray seated in front
of her typewriter in an office,
1976-1977.

The candidates for ordination
kneeling on kneelers, flanking
the Bishop, 1977. Pauli
Murray bottom left.

Pauli Murray standing at a
lectern, 1977-1980.

Pauli Murray a few days
before ordination to the
priesthood, 1977.

Portrait of Murray seated
in front of a Magnolia tree,
1978.

Hope is a song in a weary throat.

Give me a song of hope
And a world where I can sing it.
Give me a song of faith
And a people to believe in it.
Give me a song of kindliness
And a country where I can live it.
Give me a song of hope and love
And a brown girl's heart to hear it.[148]

—Pauli Murray, "Dark Testament"

AUTHORS' NOTES

Rosita Stevens-Holsey

It has been acknowledged that Pauli Murray performed a tremendous amount of ideological research and wrote, profoundly, against the unfair, illegal, and unjust civil rights practices of her day. Her works, specifically as an activist, attorney, and priest are now being uncovered, rendering her life and legacy stronger and more relevant. As one of Pauli Murray's nieces, the daughter of her youngest sister, Rosetta Murray Stevens, I not only feel it is an honor to be part of enhancing and promoting her legacy but my responsibility as a family member to do so. Aunt Pauli and I developed a unique closeness, although we usually lived miles apart. I was a part of her "Washington, D.C., family headquarters," her home away from home. I cherish my memories of her visits to D.C., as well as my being able to visit with her and accompany her on outings with important dignitaries. I was deeply influenced by her independence, perseverance, determination, and strong will. During my formative years she instilled in me a strong sense of being an advocate, activist, and young feminist teenager. As an emerging woman, Aunt Pauli supported me by letting me live in her apartment in New York City when I began my career. Throughout my life I followed her lead in advocating for human rights issues and fighting discrimination against women, minorities, and those in need. Part of my current work is to support and enhance organizations' efforts to promote my aunt's legacy by speaking and personal appearances. I am a contributor and supporter of the Pauli Murray Center for History and Social Justice in Durham, North Carolina. The Center's building was originally the family's ancestral home, which was designated a National Treasure in 2015 and a National Historic Landmark by the Department of the Interior in 2017. The world is beginning to know of Aunt Pauli and her pioneering work. Books for adults on the work of the Reverend Dr. Pauli Murray have been written. Now it is time to bring Aunt Pauli's story to young minds and challenge them to follow in her footsteps in the continuing fight for equality and human rights. My hope, as a teacher, is to be the one to do that.

Co-Author Rosita Stevens with a tricycle
in Cheyenne, Wyoming, found among
Pauli Murray's photographs.

Terry Catasús Jennings

I found Pauli Murray during my research for The Women's Liberation Movement: 1960–1990. As I got to know her work, I found that she was as large a force for the advancement of civil rights as she had been for women's rights. The "firsts" in her life and the barriers she broke were critical to both movements. I am honored to help "those who come after" hear her epic story.

ACKNOWLEDGEMENTS

The authors would like to thank the Pauli Murray Estate, Karen Ross, and Charlotte Sheedy for the use of the photographs in this book. Laura Peimer, Tom Lingner, and The Schlesinger Library's Harvard Radcliffe Institute were invaluable in our research and obtaining documents and photographs. Thanks to Barbara Lau from the Pauli Murray Center for her support and encouragement, and to Tony Whitehead for his expert advice and encouragement. The writing of this book was a labor of love for both of us. Terry's critique partners pored over version after version of this manuscript. Thank you for having come on this journey. Thanks to Adryan Nash for assisting Rosita and to Danielle Holley-Walker at Howard University Law School for her help in obtaining documents for our book. Our agent, Natalie Lakosil, guided us through many iterations of this project and our editor, Courtney Fahy, and the team at Little Bee believed in the project from the minute they saw it. Courtney loved Pauli as much as we do and was committed to getting her story out to young readers. We are grateful for her enthusiasm and her good humor as our vision took shape and became a reality.

TIMELINE OF PAULI MURRAY'S LIFE

1910   Born in Baltimore, Maryland, on November 20

1926   Graduates from Hillside High School, Durham, North Carolina and moves in with Cousin Maude to attend Hunter College

1927   Back in North Carolina to work and earn money for Hunter College

1928-
1933   Attends Hunter College

1932   First article gets accepted for publication in Echo, a college magazine

1933   Gets job as a field representative for Opportunity magazine of the National Urban League

1934   Attends Camp Tera and has first interaction with Eleanor Roosevelt

1935   Becomes a teacher for the WPA Remedial Reading Project

1936   Joins the WPA Workers' Education Project

1938   Writes first letter to President Roosevelt, copy to Eleanor. Eleanor responds. Urges patience.

1939   Fired from WPA (program closes). Unemployed and has to ask for public assistance. Writes *New York Herald Tribune* and sends copy to Eleanor Roosevelt. Mrs. Roosevelt writes about it in her column "My Day."

1940   Gets job organizing National Sharecroppers Week. Speaks with Eleanor Roosevelt in person.

1940   Eleanor Roosevelt crosses picket line at movie Abe Lincoln in Illinois. Pauli writes scathing letter.

1940   Jailed in Virginia for disturbing the peace (not riding in the back of the bus).

1940   Gets job with Workers Defense League puts her in the role of raising money to mount an appeal for Odell Waller.

1940	Meets Leon Ransom of Howard Law School and Thurgood Marshall of NAACP while raising money for Odell's appeal. They talk about law school.
1941	Attends camp in the Catskills writing and giving lectures on sharecropping before entering Howard Law School.
1942	Writes "Negro Youth's Dilemma" with Pauline Redmond, discussing how difficult it is for young Black men to fight against Hitler, when they faced discrimination and lynchings back home.
1942	Odell Waller executed on July 2. Pauli organizes march in New York on July 25 to protest Waller's death.
1942	Begins close relationship with Eleanor Roosevelt. Writes scathing letter to the president. Eleanor counsels restraint and invites Pauli to tea.
1942	Meets Caroline Ware
1943	Protests to integrate the Little Palace Cafeteria on April 17
1943	Writes poem "Mr. Roosevelt Regrets" in response to the Detroit race riots in the summer. Published in NAACP's The Crisis. Followed by poem "Negroes Are Fed Up" published in Common Sense.
1943	Writes poem "Harlem Riot, 1943"
1943	Denied honor of Chief Justice of the Court of Peers at Howard Law School during her junior year.
1944	Achieves honor of Chief Justice of the Court of Peers in her senior year at Howard Law School
1944	Proposes in law school that Plessy v. Ferguson be overturned on the basis of the Fourteenth Amendment
1944	Protests to integrate a John R. Thompson Company restaurant in April
1944	Graduates top of class from Howard Law School but is denied admission and scholarship to Harvard based on gender.
1944	Writes for *PM* and the *Sentinel*. Enters Boalt Hall of Law in Berkeley, California. Writes "Dark Testament" poem published in *South Today*.

1945	Receives master's degree from Boalt Hall of Law and passes California bar exam
1945	Offered a job as a deputy attorney general of California but loses it due to appendicitis.
1946	Starts job with the Commission on Law and Social Action, an agency of the American Jew Congress.
1946	Meets Judge Dorothy Kenyon associated with the ACLU
1947	Passes bar exam in New York
1947	Unnamed attorney hires her as associate to handle cases for a percentage of fees earned. He promises to add her name to the firm but never lived up to his word or paid her all her earnings. Left job deeply in debt, which would take her twelve years to pay off.
1948	Set up her own practice. Aunt Pauline and Aunt Sallie now living with her in Brooklyn.
1949	Liberal party asks her to run for city council from the Tenth District in Brooklyn. Endorsed by the *New York Post*, Citizens Union, and Americans for Democratic Action, she does not win but does much better than expected.
1949	Women's Division of Christian Service of the Methodist Church asks her to write a book compiling info on Jim Crow laws. She is able to set up her own office on April 1.
1949	Relationship with Eleanor Roosevelt strengthens. Invited to New York apartment, to Val-Kill.
1951	States' Laws on Race and Color is published on March 5.
1952	Applies for a job with Cornell University as research assistant to the director of Codification of the Laws of Liberia. Easily the most qualified person in the United States because of her work on States' Laws on Race and Color. Rejected because of McCarthyism.
1952	Begins writing *Proud Shoes*. Receives a grant from Harper & Brothers of $2,500, which allows her to concentrate on the book.

1954	Receives a contract from Harper & Brothers and a stipend. Accepted for a "several weeks" residence at MacDowell Colony for Artists in Peterborough, New Hampshire. Meets James Baldwin, the only other Black writer accepted at the colony.
1954	Supreme Court announces the decision on *Brown v. Board of Education* on May 17.
1955–1956	Aunt Pauline passes away at eighty-five-years-old. Seven months later, Aunt Sallie dies.
1956	*Proud Shoes* is published on October 17.
1956	Hired as an associate lawyer by Paul, Weiss, Rifkind, Wharton & Garrison, a white law firm, one of the largest and most respected in the country. There she meets Renee Barlow.
1960	Moves to Ghana to teach the "first course in constitutional and administrative law to be given at the law school" in Accra, Ghana.
1961	Accepts offer of admission and scholarship for doctoral studies at Yale
1962	Becomes participant in the President's Commission on the Status of Women and a member of the Committee on Civil and Political Rights. Prepares a report titled "A Proposal to Reexamine the Applicability of the Fourteenth Amendment to State Laws and Practices Which Discriminate on the basis of Sex, Per Se."
1962	Eleanor Roosevelt passes away on November 7.
1963	The final report is submitted to the President's Commission.
1964	Pauli prepares "Memorandum in Support of Retaining the Amendment to H.R. 7152 (Equal Employment Opportunity) to Prohibit Discrimination in Employment Because of Sex."
1964	Civil Rights Act of 1964 becomes law, including prohibition for discrimination on the basis of "sex."
1965	Graduates from Yale with doctoral degree of juridical science
1965	Coauthors with Mary Eastwood "Jane Crow and the Law: Sex Discrimination and Title VII," published in the George Washington Law Review

1965	Appointed to the National Board of Directors of the ACLU. Holds the post for eight years.
1965	Asked to help write the brief for White v. Crook by the ACLU board. Works with Judge Dorothy Kenyon. Which proves that excluding women, Black and white, and Black men from juries was a violation of the Fourteenth Amendment.
1965	Gives speech before the National Council of Women and is contacted by Betty Friedan, author of *The Feminine Mystique* and an active feminist.
1966	Founding meeting of NOW, National Organization of Women. Pauli is a founding member and member of organizing committee.
1966	Becomes a consultant to EEOC, for a seven-month period
1967	Accepts administrative position as vice president for curricular development at Benedict College, a Baptist Negro college in Columbia, South Carolina to develop educational plans and programs geared toward innovative approaches that would help close the educational gap between Black college students and their white counterparts.
1968	"Dark Testament" read at Martin Luther King Jr.'s funeral. Causes her poems to be published in a book titled *Dark Testament and Other Poems* in 1970.
1968	(Summer) Joined Brandeis University, to teach an American Civilization program and helped develop Afro-American Studies Program. Prospective lawyers. Called it perhaps her most rewarding involvement.
1968	As she begins at Brandeis, Black students across the United States are protesting. As a professor, she understands and identifies with the administration of the school. As a Black person, she understands the students' plight.
1970	Appointed to a special Commission on Ordained and Licensed Ministries to study women's issues. The group was not funded by the church, so the group met and produced a report regardless. Women's ordination was in the works.

1971	Ruth Bader Ginsburg uses Pauli and Dorothy Kenyon's work to win her landmark case on gender discrimination: *Reed v. Reed*. She credits Pauli and Kenyon's work on *White v. Crook* for her win.
1972	Named Louis Stulberg Professor of Law and Politics in the American Studies Department at Brandeis. Also became a lecturer at Boston University.
1973	Renee Barlow loses use of her right hand and arm. Diagnosed with a brain tumor. She cares for Renee in her final weeks. Renne dies on February 21.
1973	Renee's death convinces Pauli that she has a calling from God to become a minister.
1973	Resigns from Brandeis. Accepts to enter the General Theological Seminary as a special student. At this time women were still not able to be ordained as priests in the Episcopal Church. Could become a deacon but not a priest.
1973	Pauli attends a ceremony where five female deacons step up to the altar to be ordained along with five male deacons but are turned away by the bishop.
1974	Eleven female deacons ordained as priests in Philadelphia without sanction of the church but in plain view and publicity.
1976	Enters Virginia Theological Seminary for her last year of study.
1976	Episcopal General Convention allows ordination of women as priests.
1977	January 8. Pauli is ordained as a priest at the Washington National Cathedral.
1977	Celebrates her first Holy Eucharist at the Chapel of the Cross, in Chapel Hill, North Carolina, the chapel where Granma Cornelia was baptized. She reads the gospel standing behind a lectern donated by Mary Ruffin Smith, her great-grandaunt. She used her grandmother's Bible and a ribbon from the Roosevelt's graduation bouquet as a marker for her readings.

1977–1985	Pauli holds posts as interim priests in churches in Washington, D.C., Pittsburgh, Baltimore, and many other locations. She continues working on her autobiography and is a lecturer and writer.
1985	Pauli dies on July 1 at seventy-four-years-old in Pittsburgh, Pennsylvania. She has not quite finished editing her autobiography, *Song in a Weary Throat*. Caroline Ware writes the epilogue for the book.

ENDNOTES

1. Pauli Murray, "Dark Testament," in *Dark Testament and Other Poems* (New York: Liveright, 2018), 19.
2. Pauli Murray, *Pauli Murray: The Autobiography of a Black Activist, Feminist, Lawyer, Priest, and Poet*, 2nd ed. (Knoxville: University of Tennessee Press, 1989), 3.
3. Anna Pauline Murray changed her name to Pauli when she went to college. As a child, her family referred to her as little Pauline. For simplicity and clarity, we have chosen to use the name she adopted in later life from the beginning.
4. Murray, *Autobiography*, 16.
5. Murray, *Autobiography*, 1.
6. Murray, *Autobiography*, 23.
7. Murray, *Autobiography*, 18.
8. Pauli Murray, *Proud Shoes: The Story of an American Family* (New York: Harper & Brothers, 1956), 32.
9. Murray, *Autobiography*, 25.
10. *Pauli Murray, Autobiography*, 76.
11. Murray, *Autobiography*, 41.
12. Murray, *Proud Shoes*, 5.
13. Murray, *Proud Shoes*, 10.
14. Murray, *Proud Shoes*, 13–16.
15. Murray, *Proud Shoes*, 16.
16. Murray, *Proud Shoes*, 21.
17. Murray, *Proud Shoes*, 51.
18. Murray, *Proud Shoes*, 33.
19. Murray, *Autobiography*, 22.
20. Murray, *Autobiography*, 25.
21. Murray would later write a book about her ancestors called *Proud Shoes*.
22. Murray, *Proud Shoes*, 112.
23. Murray, *Proud Shoes*, 112.
24. Murray, "Dark Testament," 15.
25. Murray, *Autobiography*, 45.
26. Murray, "Dark Testament," 5.
27. Murray, *Autobiography*, 46.
28. Murray, *Autobiography*, 75; "Juliette Derricotte: Dean of Women of Fisk University Denied Medical Treatment (1931)," Black Then, Blackthen.com/juliette-derricotte-dean-of-women-of-fisk-university-denied-medical-treatment-1931/.
29. Murray, *Proud Shoes*, 263.
30. Murray, *Autobiography*, 68.
31. Murray, *Autobiography*, 70.
32. Rosalind Rosenberg, *Jane Crow: The Life of Pauli Murray* (New York: Oxford University Press, 2017), 37.
33. Rosenberg, *Jane Crow*, 38.
34. Murray, *Autobiography*, 77.
35. Pauli Murray, "Psalm of Deliverance," in *Dark Testament and Other Poems* (New York: Liveright, 2018), 40.
36. Pauli Murray, interview by Genna Rae McNeil, South Oral History Program Collection, February 13, 1976, docsouth.unc.edu/sohp/G-0044/G-0044.html.
37. Pauli Murray, "The Song of the Highway," in *Dark Testament and Other Poems (New York: Liveright, 2018), 57-58. Originally published in Nancy Cunard, ed., Negro Anthology Made by Nancy Cunard, 1931–1933* (London: Nancy Cunard at Wishart & Co, 1934), 90–93.
38. Cunard, *Negro*, 90.
39. Murray, *Autobiography*, 95.

40. Murray, *Autobiography*, 96.
41. Murray, *Autobiography*, 96.
42. Rosenberg, *Jane Crow*, 49.
43. Rosenberg, *Jane Crow*, 51.
44. Murray, "Dark Testament," 3.
45. Murray, *Autobiography*, 107.
46. Murray, *Autobiography*, 107–8.
47. Murray, *Autobiography*, 99.
48. Murray, *Autobiography*, 110.
49. Murray, *Autobiography*, 123.
50. Murray, *Autobiography*, 126.
51. Pauli Murray, interview by Genna Rae McNeil.
52. Murray, "Dark Testament," 3.
53. Murray, *Autobiography*, 134.
54. Murray, *Autobiography*, 135.
55. The protest was also because the theater had sponsored a contest for an Abe Lincoln look-alike and the man who had won was a light-skinned Black man. When the theater found out he was Black, they canceled the contest and refused the man the prize. Murray, *Autobiography*, 136.
56. Murray, *Autobiography*, 136–37.
57. Murray, *Autobiography*, 138–49.
58. Murray, *Autobiography*, 144.
59. Murray, *Autobiography*, 138.
60. Rosa Parks was jailed for refusing to give her seat to a man in 1955. The NAACP defended her. Martin Luther King Jr. organized bus boycotts after this.
61. Richard B. Sherman, *The Case of Odell Waller and Virginia Justice, 1940–1942* (Knoxville: University of Tennessee Press, 1992), 3.
62. Sherman, *The Case of Odell Waller*, 10-12
63. Sherman, *The Case of Odell Waller*, 8.
64. Sherman, *The Case of Odell Waller*, 10–11.
65. Karen Cook Bell, "Gender, Civil Rights, and the Case of Odell Waller," *Black Perspectives* (blog), *AAIHS*, February 26, 2018, www.aaihs.org/gender-civil-rights-and-the-case-of-odell-waller/.
66. Sherman, *The Case of Odell Waller*, 10–11.
67. Bell, "Gender, Civil Rights, and the Case of Odell Waller."
68. Bell, "Gender, Civil Rights, and the Case of Odell Waller."
69. Sherman, *The Case of Odell Waller*, 15.
70. Murray, "Dark Testament," 15.
71. Bell, "Gender, Civil Rights, and the Case of Odell Waller."
72. Sherman, *The Case of Odell Waller*, 32.
73. Murray, *Autobiography*, 156.
74. Murray, *Autobiography*, 172–73.
75. Murray, *Autobiography*, 173-74
76. Murray, "Dark Testament," 16.
77. Murray, *Autobiography*, 175–76
78. Ransom was the recruiter for Howard University School of Law at the time. Pauli did not know that.
79. Murray, *Autobiography*, 181.
80. Both Black and white women would not gain the vote until 1920, when the Nineteenth Amendment was ratified.
81. Thurgood Marshall, who later became the first Black justice of the Supreme Court, graduated from Howard Law School. He was a lawyer for the NAACP. Spottswood Robinson III graduated from Howard Law School a few years before Pauli with the best grades achieved to

date. He became a professor at Howard Law School. Ransom was the dean of Howard Law School at the time Pauli studied there. He rose from instructor to professor to dean at the university. All the men were part of the legal staff for the NAACP. Both Marshall and Robinson participated in *Brown v. Board of Education of Topeka, Kansas.*

82. Murray, *Autobiography*, 221.

83. Murray, *Autobiography*, 207–9.

84. Pauli Murray, "The Newer Cry," in *Dark Testament and Other Poems* (New York: Liveright, 2018), 50.

85. Pledge signed by participants in Murray, *Autobiography*, 223.

86. Pickets read: "Are You for HITLER's Way (Race Supremacy) or the AMERICAN Way (Equality)? Make Up Your Mind!"; "We Die Together. Why Can't We Eat Together?" Murray, *Autobiography*, 224.

87. Article in the New York *People's Voice decries these actions. Article excerpt in Murray, Autobiography*, 227. The Howard Chapter of NAACP went against it. See Murray, *Autobiography*, 227–28.

88. Murray, *Autobiography*, 200.

89. Murray, *Autobiography*, 183.

90. Murray, *Autobiography*, 184. There was one other woman in the incoming class who only lasted through the first semester. A total of four women were in the law school during Pauli's time there.

91. Murray, *Autobiography*, 184.

92. Murray, *Autobiography*, 184.

93. Murray, *Autobiography*, 221.

94. Murray, *Autobiography*, 221.

95. Murray, *Autobiography*, 222.

96. Murray, *Autobiography*, 238.

97. Murray, *Autobiography*, 239.

98. Murray, *Autobiography*, 244.

99. Murray, *Autobiography*, 243.

100. Boalt Memorial Hall of Law was the home of the UC Berkeley School of Law. In January 2020, the University severed all ties to the namesake of the school, John Boalt, for racism and bigotry against Chinese immigrants.

101. Rosenberg, *Jane Crow*, 141.

102. Murray, *Autobiography*, 244.

103. Pauli couldn't help herself. It must have been the devil sitting on her shoulder who made her write the Governor of Virginia, the one who didn't stop Odell Waller's death, to tell him of her graduation. "A live lawyer [is] far more danger to [your] system than a dead sharecropper."

104. Murray, *Autobiography*, 251. One day in hopes to getting to Denver to pick up money from PM to get new tires, they started driving at 3 a.m. By midafternoon, the searing sun baked them, the tires were thinning, and Pauli was determined not to spend one more night before getting to Denver. Frayed tempers flared. Mildred accused Pauli of driving her car to the ground and Pauli, in a huff, put on the brakes and got out of the car. Mildred left her. Alone, scared, thirsty, and with two dollars in her pocket, Pauli walked west. She eventually found a ride that she could trust, until, hours later, Mildred's

little white car came back to get her.

105. Murray, *Autobiography*, 253.
106. Murray, *Autobiography*, 254.
107. Murray, *Autobiography*, 253.
108. Rosenberg, *Jane Crow*, 149. The basis for Pauli Murray's conclusions was Gunnar Myrdal's book *An American Dilemma*, which included many studies and essays on the race problem in the United States.
109. Rosenberg, *Jane Crow*, 145-150.
110. Murray, *Autobiography*, 254-55.
111. Murray, *Autobiography*, 254.
112. In this instance Pauli Murray was addressing constitutionality based on the Thirteenth Amendment.
113. The justices that handed down *PvF* may very possibly have been biased against dark skin.
114. Murray, *Autobiography*, 242.
115. "An American Credo" appeared in *Common Ground* magazine. Quote from the *Catholic Digest*, April 1945, No. 6. Obtained at Schlesinger Library. This is condensed from *Common Ground* by Pauli Murray herself.
116. Murray, *Autobiography*, 256.
117. Murray, *Autobiography*, 277.
118. Murray, *Autobiography*, 285.
119. Murray, *Autobiography*, 284-285.
120. Murray, *Autobiography*, 285.
121. Murray, *Autobiography*, 289.
122. Murray, *Autobiography*, 311.
123. Pauli Murray, "Psalm of Deliverance," 36.
124. Rosenberg, *Jane Crow*, 195.
125. Murray, *Autobiography*, 255.
126. Rosenberg, *Jane Crow*, 195.
127. Murray, *Autobiography*, 255.
128. "Little Rock Nine," *History.com*, updated February 10, 2020, www.history.com/topics/black-history/central-high-school-integration.
129. "Greensboro Sit-In," *History.com*, updated March 29, 2021, www.history.com/topics/black-history/the-greensboro-sit-in.
130. "Civil Rights Activist James Meredith Shot," *History.com*, www.history.com/this-day-in-history/james-meredith-shot.
131. Murray, Dark Testament, "Psalm of Deliverance," 37.
132. Letter to Caroline Ware, sources 5.264, 7.109.
133. Jennifer Scanlon, "Where Were the Women in the March on Washington?" *The New Republic*, March 16, 2017, newrepublic.com/article/131587/women-march-washington.
134. John Adams, "Ten Things to Know about the March on Washington," Learning for Justice, August 28, 2012, learningforjustice.org/magazine/ten-things-to-know-about-the-march-on-washington.
135. The Eisenhower administration would point to happy women in the home with all their new postwar gadgets as a sign that the U.S. was better than the Soviet Union. Terry Catasús Jennings, *The Women's Liberation Movement, 1960–1990* (Broomall, PA: Mason Crest, 2013), 18.
136. Betty Friedan, *The Feminine Mystique* (New York: W. W. Norton, 1963), 21. Also see Betty Friedan, "Up from the Kitchen

Floor," *New York Times*, March 4, 1973: "We didn't admit to each other if we felt there should be more in life than peanut butter sandwiches with the kids, if throwing powder into the washing machine didn't make us relive our wedding night, if getting the socks or shirts pure white was not exactly a peak experience, even if we did feel guilty about the tattle-tale gray."

137. Murray, *Autobiography*, 349.
138. Looking back, to a visit to Val Kill, Pauli felt she should have known something was wrong when Mrs. Roosevelt asked her to fetch her a glass of lemonade rather than getting it herself. It was the last time Pauli saw The First Lady alive. Pauli lost a

dear friend, a mentor, an aunt, a mother, all rolled up into one. "She filled the landscape of my adult life." The oppressed lost a most powerful champion. The world lost its First Lady. Murray, Pauli. *Autobiography,* 350-351.
139. Pauli Murray preferred the use of Negro, but Black became common usage around the time of the civil rights movement.
140. Murray, *Autobiography*, 357.
141. Murray, *Autobiography*, 365.
142. Murray, *Autobiography*, 366.
143. Murray, *Autobiography*, 368.
144. Jennings, *The Women's Liberation Movement*, 36.
145. Troy R. Saxby, *Pauli Murray: A Personal and Political Life* (Chapel Hill: The University of North Carolina Press, 2020), 57.
146. Murray, *Autobiography*, 316.
147. Murray, *Autobiography*, 48.
148. Murray, "Dark Testament," 13.

BIBLIOGRAPHY

Adams, John. "Ten Things to Know about the March on Washington," *Learning for Justice,* August 28, 2012. Accessed April 15, 2019. https://www. learningforjustice.org/magazine/ten-things-to-know-about-the-march-on-washington.

Americanhistory.si.edu. "White Only: Jim Crow in America." Separate is Not Equal Brown v. Board of Education. Smithsonian website, http://americanhistory.si.edu/brown/history/1-segregated/white-only-1. html.

Andrews, Kelly U. "Identity and Discrimination in the Transgender Culture: Advocacy Through the Lens of Mental Health." Thesis Paper, Regis University, 2016.

Asbury, Edith Evans. "Protest Proposed on Women's Jobs." *The New York Times,* October 13, 1965. Accessed January 14, 2021. https:// timesmachine.nytimes.com/timesmachine/1965/10/13/95911829. pdf?pdf_redirect=true&ip=0

Austin, Lewis, "Jim Crow Bus Dispute Leads to Girls Arrest," *Carolina Times,* April 6, 1940, https://newspapers.digitalnc.org/lccn/sn83045120/1940-04-06/ed-1/.

Bate, Marisa. "Born to Protest: Trail Blazer Pauli Murray Takes Her Rightful Place in History." Bitch Media. December 20, 2018, file:///Users/ anajennings/Documents/Mom's%20Essays/Pauli%20Murray/Pauli%20 Murray%20Doc/"On%20the%20Basis%20of%20Sex"%20Explores%20 Pauli%20Murray's%20Influence%20on%20RBG%20%7C%20Bitch%20 Media.webarchive

Blau, Eleanor. "63 and an activist, She Hopes to Become an Episcopal Priest." *The New York Times,* February 11, 1974.

Bell, Karen Cook. "Gender, Civil Rights, and the Case of Odell Waller," *Black Perspectives* (blog), African American Intellectual History Society, February 26, 2018, https://www.aaihs.org/gender-civil-rights-and-the-case-of-odell-waller/.

Bell-Scott, Patricia. *The Firebrand and the First Lady: Portrait of a Friendship: Pauli*

Murray, Eleanor Roosevelt, and the Struggle for Social Justice. New York: Knopf, 2016.

Blagg, Deborah. "Pauli Murray: A One Woman Civil Rights Movement." Schlesinger Newsletter. Accessed November 10, 2016. https://www.radcliffe. harvard.edu/news/schlesinger-newsletter/pauli-murray-one-woman-civil-rights-movement

Boston, Nicholas and Hallam, Jennifer. "The Slave Experience, Freedom and Emancipation." Slavery and the Making of America." Accessed on November 21, 2016. WNET. http://www.pbs.org/wnet/slavery/experience/freedom/history.html

Branch, Taylor. "Globalizing King's Legacy." *The New York Times.* January 16, 2006. Accessed February 20, 2014. http://www.nytimes.com/2006/01/16/opinion/16branch.html?p...

Collins, Gail. "The Women Behind the Men" *The New York Times.* September 22, 2007. Accessed February 20, 2014.

Cooper, Brittney. "Black, queer, feminist, erased from history: Meet the most important legal scholar you've likely never heard of." Salon.com. Wednesday, Feb 18, 2015. Accessed November 19, 2016. http://www.salon.com/2015/02/18/black_queer_feminist_erased_from_history_meet_the_most_important_legal_scholar_youve_likely_never_heard_of/

Cunard, Nancy, ed. *Negro Anthology 1931-1934.* London: Nancy Cunard at Wishart, 1934. (This is the citation for the book, but it was accessed on-line. Following is the citation for the on-line manuscript.)

"Negro anthology" New York Public Library Digital Collections. Accessed June 13, 2019. http://digitalcollections.nypl.org/items/294108d0-4abd-0134-e9a7-00505686a51c

Delmont, Matthew. "Why African-American Soldiers Saw World War II as a Two-Front Battle." Smithsonianmag.com, August 24, 2017. Accessed February 20, 2018. https://www.smithsonianmag.com/history/why-african-american-soldiers-saw-world-war-ii-two-front-battle-180964616/

Douglas, Davison M. Foreword in Murray, Pauli, Editor. *States' Laws on Race and Color.* Athens, Ga.: University of Georgia Press, 1997 (originally published in 1951 by the Women's Division of Christian Service.)

Downs, Kenya. The Black Queer, Feminist Legal Trailblazer You Never Heard Of. Code Switch. February 19, 2015. https://www.npr.org/sections/codeswitch/2015/02/19/387200033/the-black-queer-feminist-legal-trailblazer-youve-never-heard-of

Ferris.edu. "The Origins of Jim Crow." Accessed January 21, 2017. http://www.ferris.edu/HTMLS/news/jimcrow/origins.htm

Forte, David F. "Poll Taxes." "Poll Taxes." Heritage.org. Accessed November 12, 2017 http://www.heritage.org/constitution/#!/amendments/24/essays/186/poll-taxes

Foss, Sonja. "Activist for Human Liberation." in Women Public Speakers in the United States. Karlyn Kohrs Campbell, Editor. University of Virginia: Greenwood Press, 1993. Accessed as e-book November 11, 2017.

Freedman, Estelle B., editor. *The Essential Feminist Reader.* New York: The Modern Library (Random House), 2007. [Murray, Pauli. *Testimony, House Committee on Education and Labor, US, 1970.]*

Friedan, Betty. "Up from the Kitchen Floor." *The New York Times*, March 4, 1973.

Gates, Henry Louis. Originally posted on The Root. "What Was Black America's Double War?" Accessed February 7, 2018. http://www.pbs.org/wnet/african-americans-many-rivers-to-cross/history/what-was-black-americas-double-war/

Gilmore, Glenda Elizabeth. *Defying Dixie: The Radical Roots of Civil Rights 1919-1950.* New York: Norton and Company, 2008.

Government Publishing Office. "Amendments to the Constitution of the United States of America. Accessed November 18, 2016. https://www.gpo.gov/fdsys/pkg/GPO-CONAN-1992/pdf/GPO-CONAN-1992-7.pdf

History.com. "Civil Rights Activist James Meredith Shot," February 9, 2010. Accessed February 25, 2021. https://www.history.com/this-day-in-history/james-meredith-shot.

History.com. "Greensboro Sit-In,", February 4, 2010. Accessed February 25, 2021. https://www.history.com/topics/black-history/the-greensboro-sit-in.

History.com. "The Compromise of 1877." March 17, 2011. Accessed November 21, 2016. http://www.history.com/topics/us-presidents/compromise-of-1877

History.com. "Little Rock Nine," January 29, 2010. Updated February 10, 2020. Accessed, February 25, 2021. https://www.history.com/topics/black-history/central-high-school-integration.

Isserman, Maurice. "Pathfinders". Review of Defying Dixie by Glenda Gilmore. *The New York Times,* February 10, 2008.

Jennings, Terry Catasús. *The Women's Liberation Movement, 1960-1990.* Philadelphia: Mason Crest, 2013.

Jones, Jae. "Juliette Derricotte: Dean of Women of Fisk University Denied Medical Treatment (1931). BlackThen.com. Posted on September 5, 2017. Accessed August 24, 2018. https://blackthen.com/juliette-derricotte-dean-of-women-of-fisk-university-denied-medical-treatment-1931/

Kshs.org. "Brown v. The Board of Education: The Case of the Century." Kansas Bar Association. 2004 Accessed August 18, 2018.

Lash, Joseph P. *Eleanor and Franklin.* New York: Norton and Company, 1971.

Law.justia.com. "White v. Crook, 251 F. Supp. 401 (M.D. Ala. 1966)" https://law.justia.com/cases/federal/district-courts/FSupp/251/401/2249435/.

Lazarus, Lillian G. "Pauli Murray's Life." *The New York Times.* April 26 1987. Accessed November 21, 2016. http://www.nytimes.com/1987/04/26/books/l-pauli-murray-s-lif...

Lear, Martha Wienman. "The Second Feminist Wave." *The New York Times,* March 10, 1968. Accessed, February 20, 2014.

Loc.gov. "The Civil War." The African American Odyssey: A Quest for Full Citizenship. Accessed November 9, 2017. https://www.loc.gov/exhibits/african-american-odyssey/civil-war.html.

Loc.gov. "Reconstruction and Its Aftermath." The African American

Odyssey: A Quest for Full Citizenship. Accessed November 9, 2017.
https://www.loc.gov/exhibits/african-american-odyssey/reconstruction.html.

McBride, Alex. "Plessy v. Ferguson 1896". Landmark Cases. Accessed
November 24, 2016.
http://www.pbs.org/wnet/supremecourt/antebellum/landmark_plessy.html

McNeil, Genna Rae, Oral Histories of the American South, UNC Chapel
Hill South Oral History Program Collection, February 13, 1976, Accessed
November 11, 2017. https://docsouth.unc.edu/sohp/G-0044/G-0044.html.

Millhiser, Ian. "'Borwn v. Board of Education' Didn't End Segregation, Big
Government Did." The Nation, May 14, 2014. Accessed November 16, 2017.
https://www.thenation.com/article/brown-v-board-education-didnt-end-
segregation-big-government-did/

Murray, Pauli. *The Autobiography of a Black Activist, Feminist, Lawyer, Priest and
Poet.* 2nd Ed. Knoxville: The University of Tennessee Press, 1987. *(*Formerly
Titled: *Song in a Weary Throat: An American Pilgrimage)*

Murray, Pauli. *Proud Shoes, The Story of an American Family.* Boston,
Massachusetts: Beacon Press, 1956.

Murray, Pauli. "The Historical Development of Race Laws in the United
States." *The Journal of Negro Education,* Vol. 22, N. 1 (Winter, 1953), pp 4-15.
Accessed November 14, 2016. URL http://www.jstor.org/stable/2293619

Murray, Pauli. *Dark Testament and Other Poems*: Liveright Publishing
Corporation, A Division of W.W. Norton & Company, New York: 2018.

Murray, Pauli. "Futility of WPA Jobs" *The New York Times.* December 5, 1938.

Murray, Pauli. "School Decision Discussed." *The New York Times,* 1954.

Murray, Pauli. "Available for Court." *The New York Times,* September 28,
1971. Accessed February 20, 2014.

Murray, Pauli. "American Credo." "Common Ground." Winter, 1944. P.
22-24.

Murray, Pauli. "Challenge to US." *The New York Times,* September 13, 1942.

Murray, Pauli. "Negro's Multiple Origins." *The New York Times*, August 3, 1968. Accessed February 20, 2014.

Murray, Pauli. "Three Thousand Miles on a Dime in Ten Days." *Negro Anthology 1931-1934*. London: Nancy Cunard at Wishart, 1934.

Pauli Murray Papers, Radcliffe Sources. 5.264, 7.109. (Letter to Caroline Ware)

Murray, Pauli and Eastburg, Mary O. "Jane Crow and the Law: Sex Discrimination and Title VII". The George Washington Law Review, Washington, DC, 1965, Volume 34, Number 2 December 1965.

Murray, Pauli. (editor). *States Laws on Race and Color*. Cincinnatti: The Woman's Division of Christian Service, The Methodist Church, 1951.

NCSU.edu. "Recruitment and Enlistment." Civil War Era NC. Accessed November 9, 2017. Rechttps://cwnc.omeka.chass.ncsu.edu/exhibits/show/35th-usct/soldiers/enlistment

Olson, Lynne. Freedom's Daughters, The Unsung Heroines of the Civil Rights Movement from 1830 to 1970. Chapter 1. Scribner, 2001. In New York Times on the Web. Accessed November 19, 2016. http://www.nytimes.com/books/first/o/olson-daughters.html

Ourdocuments.gov. "War Department General Order 143: Creation of the U.S. Colored Troops (1863) https://www.ourdocuments.gov/docphp?flash=false&doc=35

Oylboke, Amen, "Meet the Feminist Trail Blazer Behind 'Brown v. Board of Education' You've Probably Never Heard Of." Bustle.com, October 13, 2017. https://www.bustle.com/p/how-feminist-pauli-murray-quietly-helped-thurgood-marshall-win-brown-v-board-of-education-2796596

PBS.org. "Emancipation Proclamation." Africans in America. Accessed November 21, 2016. http://www.pbs.org/wgbh/aia/part4/4h1549t.html.

Pinn, Anthony B., editor. *Pauli Murray, Selected Sermons and Writing*. Maryknoll, New York: Orbis Books, 1970.

Oyez.org. "Reed v. Reed,", https://www.oyez.org/cases/1971/70-4. Accessed January 14, 2021.

Rosenberg, Rosalind, *Jane Crow: The Life of Pauli Murray*. New York: Oxford University Press, 2017.

Salovey, Peter. Free Speech Personified. *The New York Times*, November 26, 2017. Accessed December 21, 2017. https://www.nytimes.com/2017/11/26/opinion/free-speech-yale-civil-rights.html?_r=0

Saxby, Troy R. *Pauli Murray: A Personal and Political Life*. Chapel Hill: The University of North Carolina Press, 2020.

Scanlon, Jennifer. "Where Were the Women in the March on Washington?" *The New Republic*, March 16, 2016, https://newrepublic.com/article/131587/women-march-washington.

Schulz, Kathryn. "The Many Lives of Pauli Murray." Review of *Jane Crow: The Life of Pauli Murray* by Rosalind Rosenberg. *The New Yorker*, April 17, 2017. Accessed December 21, 2017. https://www.newyorker.com/magazine/2017/04/17/the-many-lives-of-pauli-murray

Scott, Ann Firor (editor). *Pauli Murray and Caroline Ware*. Chapel Hill: University of North Carolina Press, 2006.

Scott, Patricia Bell. *The Firebrand and the First Lady, Portrait of a Friendship*. New York: Knopf, 2016.

Sheinkin, Steve. *The Port Chicago 50: Disaster, Mutiny and the Fight for Civil Rights*. New York: Roaring Brook Press, 2014.

Sherman, Richard B. *The Case of Odell Waller and Virginia Justice, 1940–1942*. Knoxville: University of Tennessee Press, 1992.

Sinha, Manisha. "African Americans and Emancipation." Emancipation and War. Accessed November 10, 2017. https://www.gilderlehrman.org/history-by-era/african-americans-and-emancipation/essays/african-americans-and-emancipation.

The Crisis, College and School News December, 1939. Shows appointment of Suzie Elliott to be Dean of Women at Howard University. Accessed April 2, 2019. https://books.google.com/